Isla

ISLAM vs. ISIS

Why the True Islam is the exact opposite of the Islamic State

By

David Stansfield

SULBY HALL
PUBLISHERS

David Stansfield

Copyright © David Stansfield 2016

All rights reserved.
The use of any part of this publication reproduced, transmitted in any form or by any means, electronic, mechanical, photocopying, recording or otherwise stored in a retrieval system, without the express written consent of the publisher, is an infringement of the copyright law.

Islam vs. ISIS/David Stansfield

ISBN-13: 978-1537077857
ISBN-10: 1537077856

SULBY HALL PUBLISHERS

www.sulbyhall.com

Cover and book design by Denise Boiteau & David Stansfield

Printed in the United States of America

Dear honorable brother David,

This is one of my favorite books to read. It is an exceptionally well presented, timely and much needed work. As I read it, I gain light and grace from it. Thank you, David.

Rumi said that when one looks at an admirable bouquet, one must think of the gardeners who planted the seed, watered and cared constantly without knowing of results – results are from the generosity of Nature.

You inspire me, you are our hero.

May your pen have more power and you have peace, health and success.

Most respectfully,
Khizr Khan

David Stansfield

David Stansfield graduated Summa Cum Laude in Modern Arabic Studies from Durham University, and continued studying the language and the culture at the universities of Cambridge, Paris and Toronto (with Marshall McLuhan), whereupon he was recruited by MI6, the British equivalent of the CIA.

He has lived and worked in many parts of the Middle East, from Algeria, Egypt, the West Bank, and Jordan to Syria, Lebanon, Kuwait, Qatar, Bahrain, Oman, the United Arab Emirates and Iran.

David's 14-part Columbia University PBS television series, "The Middle East" was a selection in the 1987 Academy Awards Best Educational Documentary category.

Most recently, he was the Arabic consultant on the Netflix "House of Cards" television series.

David Stansfield

Authors' Note

Most of the English "interpretations" of the original Arabic of the Koran used throughout this book are by the author's academic adviser at Pembroke College, Cambridge, Professor Arthur John Arberry. See *The Koran Interpreted*, 1955, acknowledged as one of the most authentic English versions by a non-Muslim scholar. The title respects the orthodox Islamic view that the Koran cannot be translated, merely interpreted.

The remaining interpretations of the Arabic original were selected by the author from the following sources:

- Sahih International, edited by A.B. al-Mehri
- Mohammed Marmaduke Pickthall
- Abdullah Yusuf Ali
- Muhammad Habib Shakir
- Sheikh Muhammad Sarwar
- Muhammad Mohsin Khan

In addition, where it seemed appropriate to aid comprehension, the author has included some of his own interpretations of certain key Arabic words and phrases.

David Stansfield

In the Name of God, the Compassionate, the Merciful
Praise be to God, Lord of the Worlds,
Peace and Blessings be upon the Seal of the Prophets
and Messengers

Verily, humankind is in loss. Save those who believe
and do good works, and exhort one another to truth
and exhort one another to endurance.
Al-Qur'ān, 103: 2-3

We did not send you, except as a mercy to
all the worlds.
Al-Qur'ān, 21: 107

David Stansfield

TABLE OF CONTENTS

Prologue
1. Islam vs. ISIS
2. Roots of ISIS
3. What does ISIS want?
4. How does ISIS attract followers?
5. What motivates people to fight for ISIS?
6. Why is ISIS so barbaric?
7. Islam and ISIS Women
8. The growing threat of ISIS
9. Other Islamic terror organizations
10. How to defeat ISIS

David Stansfield

PROLOGUE

This book traces the history of Islam and the roots of ISIS, explaining what it wants, how it recruits its followers, and why it is so barbaric. We quote Koranic chapter and verse (in both Arabic and English) to show how every diabolical "punishment" ISIS inflicts on others is not only in flat contradiction of the Holy Book, but threatens to destroy the world's second largest religion. Throughout, we stress that it is only Muslims themselves who can rid the world of this terrible scourge.

As we address our readers directly in chapter 10, our final exhortation refers to Malala Yousafzai:

You are 23% of the world, 99% of the true Muslims pitted against the 1% of false ones. If ever the odds were stacked in a people's favor in their battle against the evil that is ISIS, they are stacked in yours. Consider what one little Muslim girl who had half her face almost blown away by a Taliban bullet has accomplished.

If Malala can persuade the Pakistan government to pass its first Right To Free Education Bill for all girls and boys, just imagine what nearly 1.6 billion Malala's could do to vanquish ISIS once and for all.

David Stansfield

1. Islam vs. ISIS

Why is the true Islam the diametric opposite of the Islamic State?

This is the question that is the heart and soul of this book. To begin to answer it, we have to go back over fourteen hundred years to 610 A.D. and a cave near the city of Mecca in what is now Saudi Arabia...

...where an Arab man by the name of Muhammad has just been visited by the Angel Gabriel.

Gabriel asks Muhammad to recite a series of verses, which he assures him come directly from God.

Over the next twenty-two years, this angel is to visit Muhammad again and again with more and more verses from God for him to recite, all of which are subsequently to be chunked together into "The "Recitation," *al-Qur'ān*, or Koran as we mangle it.

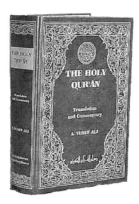

All Muslims have to believe that all we know of what God has ever said to mankind is in the Koran as dictated by God via the Angel Gabriel to the man who became known as the Prophet – or the Messenger – Muhammad. That's it. Period. This stretch of time, between 610 and 632 A.D., is the ONLY stretch of time during which God has spoken to humanity, since the universe began. All the rest is hearsay.

Several verses of the Koran stand out from the rest because they contain the first ever appearances of the word *Muslim*. Here's an example:

> We are supporters of God. We have believed in God and testify that we are Muslims.
> *[meaning "One who submits to God]*

A note about the Arabic language: almost all words are derived from a basic three-letter Semitic root verb, which can branch out into a number of different meanings. This is the case of ***sa-li-ma***, which has to do both with submission and with peace. So while *muslim* means one who submits and *islam* means submission, *salaam* means peace, as in the standard Muslim greeting *Salaam alaykum*, Peace be upon you.

In this way, the words *Islam* and *Muslim* simultaneously connote two related concepts: submission and peace. Islam is the attainment of peace, both inner and outer peace, by the submission of oneself to the teachings of God.

This is the basis of Islam itself, the foundation of the faith of every Muslim. Precisely because God only spoke to Muhammad, and precisely because He spoke in Arabic, all Muslims have to believe every word of the following Arabic sentence, or *Shahada*, their profession of faith:

لا إله إلا الله محمد رسول الله

lā ʾilāha ʾillā-llāh, muḥammadun rasūlu-llāh
There is no god but God,
Muhammad is the messenger of God

In fact, that's all one has to say to become a Muslim in the first place: *lā ʾilāha ʾillā-llāh, muḥammadun rasūlu-llāh*.

Contrast Islam's message of peace with that of ISIS, which is about nonstop savage violence and endless war, and has the unmitigated gall to emblazon the *Shahada* on its flag:

Notice that the words *muḥammadun rasūlu-llāh* are written upside-down (because of some deluded ISIS belief that the words on the Prophet's seal were in this order), but this is strangely apt considering that everything ISIS stands for turns Islam upside-down.

To what degree do Muslims support ISIS?

Well, let's look at the numbers. Almost one in four of the world's population are Muslims; 23% to be precise, a total of 1.6 billion people. It is the world's second largest religion after Christianity, which weighs in at 2.2 billion.

Many of us automatically assume that most Muslims are concentrated in the Middle East. But this is not so.

Here's how the 1.6 billion Muslims are currently distributed across the globe, with three times as many of them living in the Asia-Pacific region as in the Middle East.

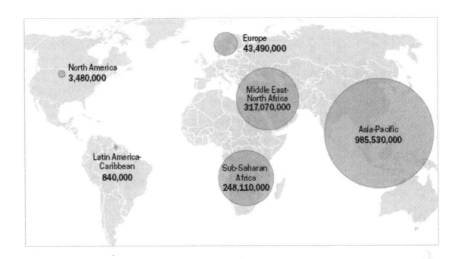

Now for the ISIS numbers. The highest estimate of the total count of ISIS fighters is around 30,000 and the latest statistics show the number of Muslims worldwide who make some claim to support ISIS ranging between 10 and 20 million. To keep our numbers simple, let's split the difference and assume that 16 million Muslim either fight for or support ISIS to one degree or another. This looks like a lot until we realize that this is only 1% of the worldwide population of 1.6 billion Muslims. all the rest of whom condemn ISIS to one degree or another. In other words…

99% of Muslims denounce ISIS

This overwhelming majority of 1,584 million Muslims who oppose ISIS can be represented by a series of concentric circles, radiating outwards from a tiny black dot standing for the 1% of Muslims who endorse ISIS.

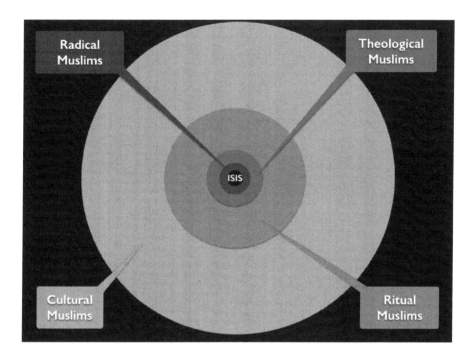

The first small, dark gray circle surrounding the ISIS dot represents radical Muslim groups such as the Muslim Brotherhood (see chapter 9); the second, slightly larger, circle stands for theological Muslims who study the Islamic texts in depth and would like to replace the law of their land with some version of the Sharia; the third, much larger, circle represents ritual Muslims, who practice the Five Pillars of Islam, but oppose the violent Sharia punishments; the fourth, and by far the largest, circle stands for Muslims who consider Islam to be part of their culture, but don't practice it regularly.

All the members of all four of the above circles – even the most radical, including the Muslim Brotherhood – have denounced ISIS with equal fervor.

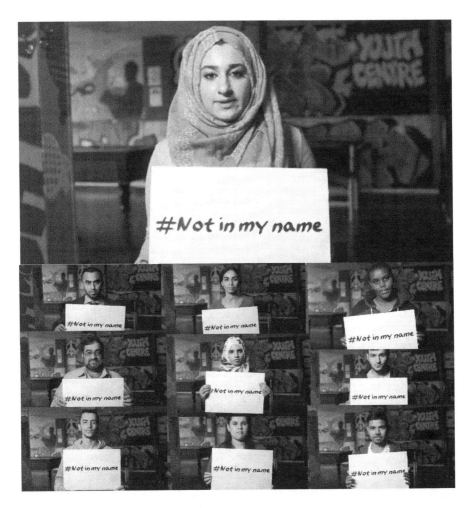

Here are some of the Islamic organizations and leaders who have taken part in this condemnation:

- **The Organization Of Islamic Cooperation**: "The Islamic State Has Nothing To Do With Islam, Has Committed Crimes That Cannot Be Tolerated."

- **Al-Azhar University, Cairo**: "The Islamic State Is Corrupt And A Danger To Islam."

- **The Arab League**: "Strongly Denounces The Crimes Against Humanity Carried Out By The Islamic State."

- **The Council on American-Islamic Relations** "Condemns The Islamic State As Un-Islamic And Morally Repugnant."

- **The Muslim Council Of Great Britain**: "Violence Has No Place In Religion."

- **The Islamic Society of North America**: "The Islamic State's Actions Are To Be Denounced And Are In No Way Representative Of What Islam Actually Teaches."

- **Saudi Arabia's Highest Religious Authority**: "The Islamic State Is The 'Number One Enemy Of Islam.'"

- **The Muslim Public Affairs Council**: "Condemns The Islamic State And Calls For A Stand Against Extremism."

Below are just a handful of the many thousands of Muslim imams and scholars from around the world who have spoken out against the Islamic State…

Joined by such Imams as these in Britain…

Islam vs. ISIS

Here, the Organization of Islamic Cooperation, representing 57 Islamic countries, gathers to denounce ISIS…

Iyad Ameen Madani, the Secretary General of the organization states that ISIS "has nothing to do with Islam and its principles that call for justice, kindness, fairness, freedom of faith and coexistence."

The rank and file of Muslims are in complete agreement...

...as are these German Muslims, who condemned ISIS in a nationwide day of prayer at several thousand mosques across the country...

...while nearly 200 Muslim scholars from around the world, seen here at a press conference in Washington D.C...

...signed an open letter to the "fighters and followers" of the Islamic State: a "point-by-point," refutation of its philosophy and the violence it has perpetrated. (See chapter 10 for more on this open letter.)

Last but by no means least is perhaps the best known and harshest of all ISIS's critics, Professor of Contemporary Islamic Studies in the Faculty of Oriental Studies at the University of Oxford, Tariq Ramadan...

...who is none other than the grandson of Hasan al-Banna, the founder of the Muslim Brotherhood.

ISIS truly is a tiny black dot, a nasty little stain on the vast fabric of Islam.

2. Roots of ISIS

Now that we have discussed the near universal contempt that the Muslim world has for ISIS, let's take a look at the twin – almost parallel – roots of this terrorist organization: Wahhabism and Imperialism, which are mutually reinforcing.

Root #1: Wahhabism.

This dates back to the early 1700s in Arabia and a man by the name of Muhammad ibn al-Wahhab, who advocated a return to the "fundamentals" of the Islamic religion as he imagined they were practiced in the time of Muhammad and the first four Caliphs.

This was an ultra strict and puritanical movement that promised death to anyone who didn't join it. "Those who would not conform to this view," declared Wahhab, "should be killed, their wives and daughters violated, and their possessions confiscated." In addition, he imposed the by now horrifically familiar list of barbaric so-called "Islamic" punishments, from beheading, amputating and stoning to crucifixion, flogging and throwing homosexuals off tall buildings, almost none of which are mentioned in the Koran, as we shall detail in chapter 6.

Eventually, al-Wahhab formed a pact with a local leader, Muhammad bin Saud, who went on to establish the "House of Saud," whose royal descendants...

...now rule almost the entire Arabian Peninsula...

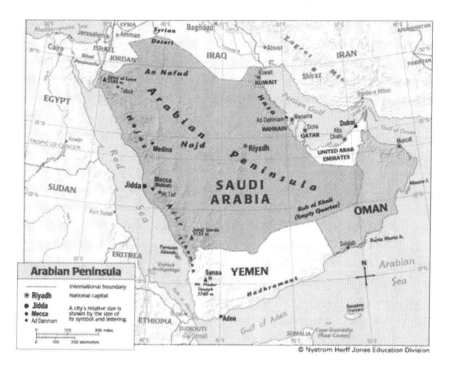

When this new kingdom was first set up in the 1920s, Saudi Arabia was one of the poorest countries on earth, eking out a living from a little agriculture and pilgrimage-to-Mecca money...

...and the extreme, fanatical Wahhabism it had inherited didn't have much effect on the outside world.

But then came the discovery of vast amounts of oil in the kingdom...

...making Saudi Arabia – almost overnight – one of the richest countries on earth.

To make themselves even richer, in 1973 the Saudis, along with the other Arab members of OPEC, Algeria, Libya, Iraq, Kuwait, Bahrain, Qatar, the United Arab Emirates, Egypt and Syria, imposed an oil embargo on the US, the UK, Japan and the Netherlands...

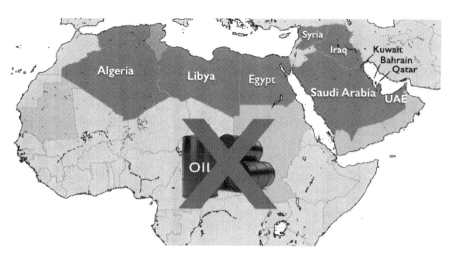

The embargo resulted in huge cutbacks in oil production on the part of OPEC, which ended up causing a 400% hike in oil prices and severe shortages of gasoline in the West and in Japan.

The upshot of all this was to propel the Arab oil exporting states, notably Saudi Arabia, Kuwait, Bahrain, Qatar and the United Arab Emirates, into a dominant position within the Muslim world.

Of all the Muslim oil states, Saudi Arabia had by far the greatest oil reserves, giving the kingdom all the billions of petrodollars it needed to export its Wahhabist form of Islam.

The kingdom promptly opened offices in every part of the world inhabited by Muslims, distributing Wahhabi translations of the Quran and Wahhabi doctrinal texts throughout the Middle East, Africa, Asia, the United States and Europe.

In all of these places, the Saudis funded the building of more than 2,000 mosques...

...complete with Wahhabi preachers, who would even perform services in the street, if all else failed...

The Saudis also established many hundreds of madrasas that provided free education for every young Muslim, again of course with the strictest possible Wahhabi curriculum…

Fast-forward to 1979, when the Soviet Union invaded Afghanistan and – according to many analysts – the CIA supplied a rich Saudi by the name of Osama bin Ladin…

…with a database of Afghani "mujahideen" (roughly translated as "guerrilla fighters") to help drive the Soviets out of their country. The Arabic name the CIA used for this database was al-Qaeda, short for *qāʿidah al-ma'lumāt* or "Base of information."

The whole exercise was a great success and the Soviets were indeed eventually driven out of that country in 1989 thanks in large part to the *jihad* waged by Osama and his men and our splendid database.

Washington apparently never dreamed that once the Soviets had withdrawn, Osama's "al-Qaeda the database" would transform itself into "al-Qaeda the terrorist movement," which would promptly turn its attention to attacking the West. But this is exactly what happened after Osama and some of his top associates met in a suburb of Peshawar, Pakistan to discuss the possibility of launching a global jihad now that the Soviets were out of the picture.

Fast-forward to 2001 and al-Qaeda's 9/11 attack on the Twin Towers (with 15 out of the 19 hijackers being Saudi citizens)…

Islam vs. ISIS

...and then to our 2003 response, which was not to invade Saudi Arabia or even al-Qaeda's headquarters in Pakistan to obliterate this new enemy, but instead to invade Iraq, the one place everyone knew did *not* harbor al-Qaeda since its secular ruler and our former ally, and Donald Rumsfeld's "good friend," Saddam Hussein, was Osama's sworn enemy.

Fast-forward again to 2007 as the raging civil war our calamitous 2003 invasion of Iraq had triggered continued to tear the country apart and inadvertently provoke exactly the opposite of what it set out to achieve by promoting the emergence of "Al-Qaeda in Iraq."

Final fast-forward to 2013 as al-Qaeda in Iraq – now based in both Syria and Iraq – rebrands itself as something much, much worse: the Islamic State in Iraq and Syria, or ISIS.

At the same time all this was going on, root #2 of ISIS, Imperialism, was coming into play.

To set the scene for this, we need to return once more to the beginnings of Islam. During the first 23 years after Muhammad's death in 632, the Muslim Empire he had founded grew at an almost unprecedented speed…

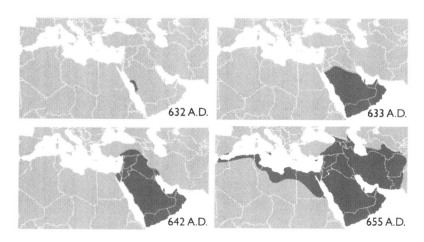

...eventually evolving into the Ottoman Empire, which at its height in the late 1600s covered this much territory...

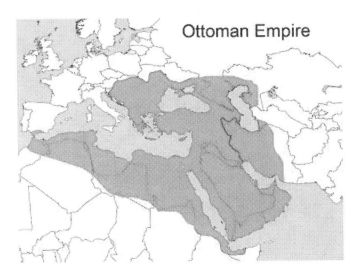

From then on, as Europe grew stronger and stronger, it was all downhill for the Ottomans. A decline that began gradually, but soon gathered more and more momentum, as one European power after another took over North Africa.

First, Napoleon occupied Egypt from 1798 to 1801...

...then the French grabbed Algeria in 1830...

...followed by Tunisia in 1881...

...and Morocco in 1912...

Islam vs. ISIS

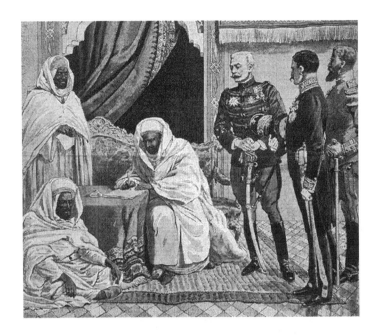

Meanwhile, the British nabbed what was to become Yemen in 1839 and snatched Egypt for themselves in 1882...

...and Italy got its hands on what would become Libya in 1912...

By 1913, The Ottoman Empire was reduced to this…

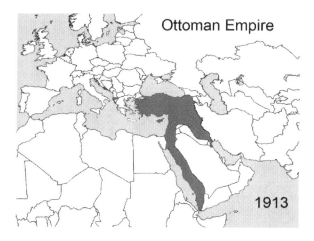

This area encompassed what is now Turkey, most of Iraq and Syria, Palestine, Jordan and western Saudi Arabia. These areas had traditionally been divided up very loosely, with fluid, constantly changing boundaries reflecting the movements of different ethnic, religious and sectarian groups of people.

Then World War One broke out and the British and the French marched in, defeated the German-backed Ottoman Turks and divided up (via the "Sykes-Picot Agreement") the central part of the Ottoman Empire between them as shown below:

Not surprisingly, this stroke of supreme imperialist arrogance immediately began to wreak havoc among the various groups of people involved as their age-old spiritual space was replaced by the deranged geometry of pencils and rulers drawing dead straight lines through ancestral tribal domains.

On top of that, the British and French colonialists, wanting to keep both the Jews and the Arabs on their side during their battles with the Ottomans, promised one particular part of the region to both peoples. This little pocket of real estate about the size of New Jersey – now named Israel or Palestine, depending which side you're on – has been a problem ever since.

The imperial hubris didn't stop there. One of the wielders of pencil and ruler was a man by the name of Winston Churchill...

...who, already celebrated for his fondness for liquid lunches, drew a sudden postprandial zigzag in the middle of the Jordanian/Saudi Arabian border that is known to this day as "Churchill's Hiccup." He even boasted that he had created Jordan "with the stroke of a pen, one Sunday afternoon in Cairo."

The Muslim world could do little more than look on helplessly as defeat piled upon defeat, humiliation upon humiliation. And resentment upon resentment.

It got worse. Here's a list of the dictatorial regimes that have sprung up in recent years (almost always with US and/or British assistance):

- Hosni Mubarak, Egypt
- Mohammad Reza Pahlavi, Iran
- Saddam Hussein, Iraq
- Bashar Al Assad, Syria
- Moammar Gaddafi, Libya
- House of Saud, Saudi Arabia
- Ali Abdullah Saleh, Yemen
- Hamad bin Isa al-Khalifa, Bahrain
- Zine El Abedine Ben Ali, Tunisia
- Jaber al-Ahmad as-Sabah, Kuwait
- Hamad bin Khalifa ath-Thani, Qatar
- Qaboos bin Said as-Said, Oman
- Muhammad bin Rashid al-Maktoum, UAE

A rogues gallery of captains and kings, emirs and sheikhs devoted to amassing the greatest amount of wealth possible, while suppressing – and when necessary, torturing and executing – their own people when they stepped out of line. More madness and more fury, building and building.

Not to mention the never-healing open wound of the Israel-Palestine conflict.

And finally, what are already proving to be the two last straws — or rather two last civil wars:

Civil War #1 in Iraq, where the aforementioned U.S. invasion of Iraq — turning Sunni against Shi'a as never before in modern times — has resulted not only in laying waste to this country...

Shock and Awe

...but in laying off 500,000 Iraqi military and civilian personnel, thousands of whom were to end up joining ISIS out of sheer desperation...

...not to mention the deaths of at least 600,000 more Iraqis...

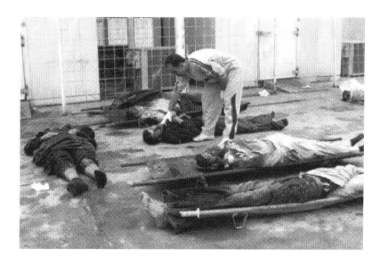

...and the internal displacement of an additional million and a half, and the external displacement of four million, the largest ever such tragedy in the Middle East...

That is, until an even greater tragedy was to take place, which brings us to...

Civil War #2 in Syria, where Bashar Al Assad...

...brutally crushed the "Arab Spring" for daring to jump up and be heard, resulting in the laying waste to that country also...

...and the deaths of nearly a quarter of a million Syrians.

Assad's lavish use of Sarin nerve gas – from three key chemical ingredients supplied by several British companies – was particularly effective...

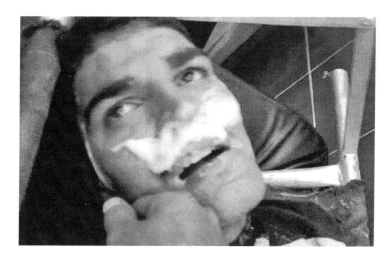

...especially on children...

...all this forcing nine million Syrians to flee their homes. That's 40% of the entire population of that country, the equivalent of 127 million Americans becoming homeless.

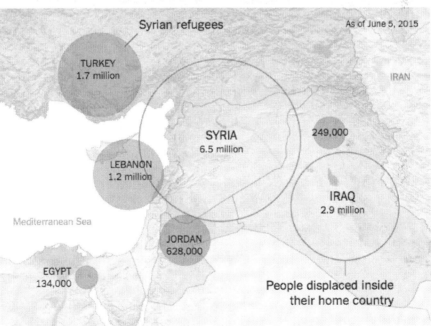

Thus was the combination of an ever more militant Wahhabism and an ever more humiliating and arrogant Imperialism and its unforeseen after effects to provide the critical mass for the ISIS explosion.

3. What does ISIS want?

Part of the answer to this lies in the name itself. As we've already said, ISIS stands for the Islamic State of Iraq and Syria. It is also referred to in English as ISL, which stands for the Islamic State of the Levant. "Levant" is the French for "rising," as in the place where the sun rises, the Eastern end of the Mediterranean, which stretches from Israel and Palestine to Iraq.

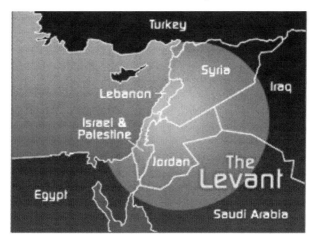

But the Arabic name of this organization gives much more meaning than the English acronym ISIS. It is الدولة الإسلامية في العراق والشام *ad-dawlat al-islamiyya fi'l-'iraq wa'sh-sham*, reduced in Arabic to the acronym *Da'ish*, "The Islamic State in Iraq and *Sham*."

The word *Sham* is the key; it resonates in the Arabic-speaker's mind on multiple levels. What does it mean? Well, one thing it does NOT mean is the truncated Syria that was created by the French after World War One. Rather, it means the "North," "Damascus," and much more tellingly, the "Greater Syria" that encompasses, not only the artificial states the British and the French carved out of the Ottoman Empire: Syria, Iraq, Lebanon, Jordan, Palestine and subsequently Israel, but also Cyprus and part of southern Turkey.

For most of the last four thousand five hundred years, nearly all of these phony modern states were one, not only under the empires of the Ottomans, the Arabs, the Byzantines, the Romans, the Greeks and the Persians, but also under the AsSYRIAns, and even more ancient civilizations before them, dating all the way back to 2,500 B.C.

Sham's roots run very deep — and dangerously — indeed, as we shall see.

However, ISIS's ambitions stretch a lot farther afield than *Sham*. Its ultimate goal is to gain control not only of the entire Middle East from Morocco to Iran...

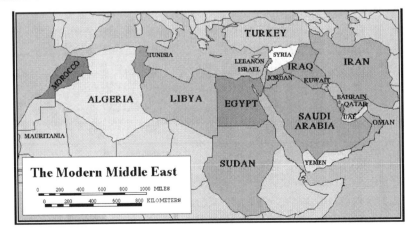

...but also of the entire Islamic world, which includes a score of African countries, numerous parts of Russia, plus Albania, Bosnia, Kosovo, Azerbaijan, Kazakhstan, Tajikistan, Turkmenistan, Uzbekistan, Afghanistan, Pakistan, Bangladesh, Malaysia, Indonesia, and substantial areas of India and China.

Why is ISIS doing this? Because its members want to set up what they call a "caliphate" over this entire world. No small feat, since as we've said, this Islamic world numbers 1.6 billion people.

What is a caliphate?

Back to the beginnings of Islam again.

Muhammad may have been the only man who ever lived whom God contacted directly, but even he couldn't live for ever. As founder of the new religion of Islam, he was eventually able to recruit enough of his fellow desert Arabs to unite most of Arabia into a single religious entity under Islam. But then in early June, 632 A.D., the Messenger fell ill with a fever and died.

The immediate question was, who would be Muhammad's successor? Or as they say in Arabic, his *khalīfah*, his caliph? Who would be the man to rule over the Messenger's succession, his *khilāfa*, his caliphate?

As it happened, the majority of the followers of Muhammad elected his father-in-law and close companion, Abu Bakr, to be Islam's first caliph. (Some of the Prophet's followers didn't agree and thought that Muhammad's son-in-law, Ali, should be the first

Caliph. Because the pro-Abu Bakr supporters called themselves *ahl as-sunnah*, the people of the tradition of Muhammad, they became known as the Sunnis. The Ali supporters, on the other hand, called themselves *shī'atu 'Alī,* the party of Ali, so they became known as the Shia or the Shiites. Today, about 85% of Muslims are Sunni and 15% are Shia.)

Leap forward in history to Iraq in 2014 and the self-appointed leader of ISIS, the Sunni Ibrahim Ali al-Badri as-Samarrai declaring himself Islam's latest caliph, conveniently changing his name to *Abu Bakr* al-Baghdadi in the process...

...as he announces ISIS's goal of taking over the world – not just the Islamic world, but the entire planet.

And not only to rule this planet, but to slaughter everyone on it who opposes the global "Islamic State" and/or doesn't subscribe to its demented version of Islam.

This list includes:

> All moderate Sunnis, plus all Shiites, Alawites, Ahmadiyyas, Ismailis, Yazidis, Druze, Kurds, Christians, Jews, Buddhists, Hindus, Jainists, Confucianists, Taoists, Copts, Greek Orthodox congregations, Maronites, Baha'ists, Sikhs, Wiccans,

Celtic polytheists, Hellenists, gypsies, atheists, and homosexuals.

all of whom are to be decapitated, shot, crucified or burned to death depending on ISIS's mood at the time.

The lunacy doesn't end there. Whippings or floggings or lashings are to be administered to everyone within ISIS's own ranks for the slightest infringement of its nonsensical rules as follows (this is just a brief sample):

- people who sing, dance, play cards or go on picnics "because they are a waste of time"
- men without long beards
- men whose trousers touch the ground
- men who smoke cigarettes or hookah pipes
- men who wear t-shirts with English writing on them
- shopkeepers who fail to close their shops or shroud the faces of their mannequins 10 minutes before prayer time
- the husbands or guardians of all women who are not wearing a full-face veil and gloves and do not refrain from raising their voices in public

In view of all of the above, how in Heaven's name does ISIS ever manage to convince *anybody* – let alone tens of thousands of people from all over the world – to want to become fighters for this horrific organisation?

4. How does ISIS attract followers?

The short answer is Propaganda.

ISIS wants it both ways: on the one hand, it wants to promote a mythical 7th century way of life at the point of a sword or a spear or a gun or a rocket or a bomb, on the other hand it wants to seduce young and old with every 21st century propaganda technique and medium known to man.

Every day, ISIS posts 90,000 social media messages, texts, blogs and images on the web via FaceBook, Twitter (50,000 accounts), Instagram, Whatsapp, Tumblr, etc., in addition to uploading endless streams of often incredibly violent videos on YouTube:

Every month, ISIS publishes a coffee-table quality online magazine in multiple languages, entitled "Dabiq," the name of a small town in northern Syria where ISIS believes the Islamic version of Armageddon will take place when the Muslim and Christian armies eventually face off against each other, with the *Muslim* army being led by Jesus Christ Himself, believe it or not.

Almost continuously, ISIS produces state-of-the-art video games inspired by such U.S. productions as "Grand Theft Auto" to recruit the young:

ISIS even employs hip-hop performers, such as the London rapper Abdel-Majed Abdel Bary, to spread its insane, poisonous message...

ISIS also produces an endless stream of online PR videos featuring small children such as these ones in Kazakhstan learning how to assemble and fire high-powered automatic weapons. No child is too small...

A recent ISIS propaganda tool to come on line is *al-Bayan* radio network (literally, "The Clearness" or "The Clarion") broadcasting in English, Arabic, French, Russian and Kurdish; the languages of the most fruitful recruiting areas. The date "1434" is from the Islamic Calendar – which begins in 622 A.D. – and is the equivalent of 2013 in our Gregorian Calendar.

Finally, in this litany of loathing, ISIS has trademarked its own iconic symbol: a single raised index finger.

Islam vs. ISIS

This is a well-known sign of power and victory around the world, but for ISIS, it has a more sinister meaning. It refers to the *tawhid*, the belief in the oneness of God. More specifically, it refers to ISIS's fundamentalist interpretation of the *tawhid*, which rejects any other view, including other Islamic interpretations, as idolatry. It affirms an ideology that demands the destruction of the West and the domination of the world.

All these are apparently irresistible messages to tens of thousands of people.

5. What motivates people to fight for ISIS?

As of January 2015, here's where most of the foreign fighters who had flocked to join ISIS came from:

Numbers & origins of non-Middle Eastern ISIS foreign fighters as of January 2015
(International Centre for the Study of Radicalisation, London, UK)

1,500	Russia	300	China
1,200	France	250	Australia
600	Germany	250	Kazakhstan
600	United Kingdom	250	Netherlands
500	Pakistan	150	Austria
500	Uzbekistan	100	Canada
460	Scandinavia	100	Spain
440	Belgium	100	USA
360	Turkmenistan	80	Italy
330	Bosnia	50	Afghanistan

Of all the possible motivations for people to want to become ISIS fighters, *madness* would seem to top the list. Are the ISIS fighters who can't wait to go around chopping people's heads off and burning them alive, all nut cases? All just crazy people? Psychopaths? Marquis de Sade in fancy dress? People who have no empathy for others, no conscience, who positively enjoy inflicting pain, who will go to any lengths to get their way in their mad lust for power?

Well, let's look at the numbers. How many psychopaths are there in the world? Experts estimate they make up about 1% of the total global population of nearly 7.4 billion people, so that means there are roughly 74 million psychopaths at large.

Does this mean there are 74 million potential ISIS recruits? Not necessarily. ISIS may seem like the perfect refuge for the psychopathic, but there are many other avenues open to such monsters. For example, in the U.S. the psychopathic rate for CEO's is 5%, and for dangerous criminals behind bars, it's 30%.

We also know from interviews that have been done with ISIS fighters that most of them are perfectly normal human beings. Here's an example of such an interview conducted by journalist Jürgen Todenhöfer with a fellow German and former Christian who'd converted to Islam to join ISIS.

This obviously highly educated and intelligent young man displayed none of the symptoms of psychopathy and yet made the following chilling pronouncements in one exchange:

Todenhöfer: "And if the Shias of Iraq and the Shias of Iran, the 150 million who live in this world, refuse to convert, it means they will be killed?"

ISIS fighter, nodding cheerfully: "Yes, exactly as we would – "

Todenhöfer: "150 million?"

ISIS fighter: "150 million, 200 million, 500 million, we don't care about the number."

Todenhöfer: "Will you kill all Muslims in Europe who don't adopt your religious beliefs?"

ISIS fighter: "He who doesn't adopt our religious beliefs, doesn't adopt Islam. And if he persists on his wrong path, then there is no option but the sword."

A psychopath? We can't know for sure. But if not, possibly someone suffering from another related mental disorder: religious mania, often diagnosed as a psychotic or schizophrenic bipolar disorder, or even epilepsy.

A second possible motivation for so many international recruits to ISIS might be termed *duality*.

To put this in context, consider why so many people drawn to ISIS are so young, such as the trio below. From left to right: Reyaad Kahn, 19, from Cardiff; Nasser Muthanna, 19, also from Cardiff; and Abdul Raqib, 19, from Aberdeen...

Reyaad Kahn was in fact only 16 when he joined the terrorist organization as shown on this still from an ISIS propaganda video...

Islam vs. ISIS

What's the great attraction? Is it just the organization's ultra sophisticated social media campaign? No. Is it simply teenage rebellion? No, again. Is it just because the caliphate sounds like such a utopian project? No, once more.

Young people are flocking to fight for ISIS for all of the above reasons of course, but first and foremost they are doing it for the same reason Harry Potter charged off to fight Voldemart...

...they are doing it for *honor*.

In numerous interviews, these youngsters say they're attracted to ISIS above all because it's…

- the right thing to do
- daring
- romantic
- what all their friends are doing, and
- just like "Call of Duty!"

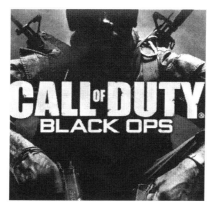

(Never mind that most of the "black ops" in the Call of Duty games target Muslims and have been banned in Saudi Arabia and the UAE)

And of course joining ISIS makes teenagers feel important; it gives meaning and importance to their often drab and dreary lives.

Another young British Muslim ISIS recruit named Ifthekar Jaman...

...summed this up well when he explained that Obama doesn't give a damn what he does for a living, but if he joins ISIS, he goes from being the manager of a second-rate British clothing store to someone giving headaches to the president of the United States.

We should note that about 15% of these foreign recruits are young women, such as these three British straight-A 15 and 16-year old students from Bethnal Green Academy in London on their way to fight for ISIS in Syria:

So it isn't only teenage boys who are drawn like flies to the ISIS light bulb, teenage girls can also be dazzled by the organization and the handsome and daring young men brandishing their Kalashnikovs…

But how can even the derring-do and the romance and the call to duty and the honor exert such a pull on these very young people that they are willing to abandon their families and their friends and their schools and their countries for a whole new life of Heaven knows what half-way across the world?

The answer is because if their own lives and environments are bad, ISIS must be good. Precisely because they are teenagers, the majority of them think in black and white terms: good guys/bad guys, Harry Potter/Voldemart, with no middle way, very little gray.

This means that their reactions to the world are very different from adult reactions. Teens make much more use of the on/off, black/white panic button in their heads known as the "amygdala," the small almond-shaped region of the brain that triggers instinctual flight or fight reactions...

Teenagers

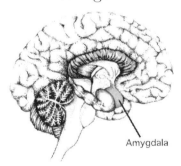

...whereas most adults make more use of the frontal cortex, which governs reason and planning: the gray areas.

Adults

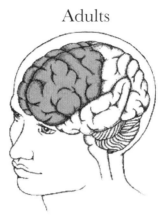

In other words, teenagers are all or nothing people, they are purists.

Now consider the ideology of ISIS: it is the ultimate in purity, its fighters the ultimate Puritans, those English Protestants who called for the purification of the Church, just as ISIS calls for the purification of Islam. No wonder so many teenagers are drawn to it. No wonder its flag is black and white.

A third motivation might be *identity*.

If you are a devout Muslim…

...here's a highly condensed and abbreviated version of what you have to do five times every day, as you prepare for your five daily prayer sessions, performing each action in the meticulously detailed prescribed fashion:

- wash both hands three times
- rinse out your mouth and throat three times
- inhale water to wash out your nose three times
- wash your face three times
- wash both arms three times
- using both your wet hands, wipe your forehead, the back of your neck and temple three times
- use your finger and thumb to clean your ears inside and out
- clean your ankles and toes three times

Repeat the above five times a day before each of your five daily prayers. If you're not sure of the correct prayer times, use one of the apps available for your cell phone or iPod.

Praying five times a day is one of the five acts or "pillars" of Islam that must be respected by all believers.

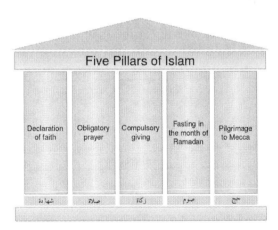

Our point here is that respecting the prayer pillar becomes especially onerous for Muslims living in the West, where most employers have little patience for their employees suddenly disappearing for extended bathroom breaks followed by equally extended face-down sessions on prayer rugs at the most inconvenient times.

Not to mention fainting from lack of food and water in the middle of the workday in the month of Ramadan.

These are just two examples of the clash that takes place all too often in many parts of Europe and North America between devout Muslims and the general populace. France's controversial prohibiting of young Muslim women from wearing headscarves and veils in public schools and universities is another.

Islam vs. ISIS

All this has created an identity crisis for many European and North American Muslims. Even if you were born in one of these regions you can still feel conflicted: am I an American – or a German or a Belgian – or am I a Muslim? Or can I be both? What am I? Whoever I am, I don't seem to be wanted here.

This confusion can be particularly intense among adolescents, who have an urgent need to develop a strong sense of identity. When this is denied them, they often seem to have no idea who or what they are, where they belong or where they want to go.

This may cause them to withdraw from normal life, or act abnormally at work, in their marriage or at school. They may even turn to negative activities, such as crime or drugs, as a way of dealing with identity crisis. To someone going through such a crisis, it is more acceptable to have a negative identity than none at all.

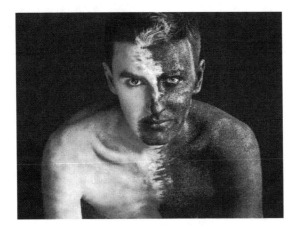

Such negativity fueled by an explosive mix of resentment and longing for acceptance combined with the racism that many Muslims encounter, especially in Britain, where their parents still have vivid memories of "Paki bashing"…

…means it's hardly surprising that many of these marginalized and alienated young men and woman become easy prey for ISIS recruiters, whether in person or over the Internet…

…who can honestly promise them all the Islam they could possibly desire (and a great deal more than they may have bargained for), along with the strongest identity imaginable as warriors for God with not a shred of doubt in their minds about the righteousness of their cause.

After all, Islam is not just something you do on Sunday mornings and at weddings and funerals; it is a complete way of life.

Fourth possible motivation: inequality.

The 62 richest people in the world now have as much wealth as the poorest 3,600,000,000 (50% of the world's population).

Such an unequal distribution of wealth has never before occurred in the history of mankind. So extraordinary is this state of affairs that a 700-page economics textbook explaining it all to us, Thomas Piketty's *Capital in the Twenty-First Century*...

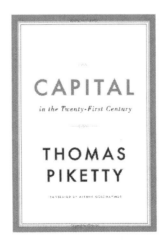

...has generated as much interest...

...and anger as Karl Marx, the father of Communism.

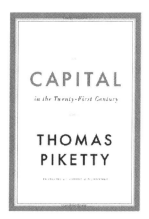 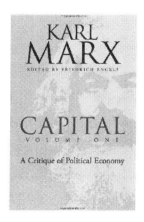

And we know what happened last time.

Could it happen here? Very likely, yes, particularly among young people. Just to take Western Europe, look at the 2014 unemployment rates for people under 25:

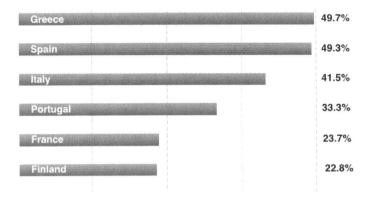

Greece	49.7%
Spain	49.3%
Italy	41.5%
Portugal	33.3%
France	23.7%
Finland	22.8%

That's an awful lot of potentially very angry and frustrated young people. All the more incensed by the super rich's continual flaunting of what their obscene mountains of money can buy: the world's largest yacht, $1.5 billion with a crew of sixty...

...the world's most expensive house, $2 billion, 27 floors, 168-car garage, 600-person staff...

...the world's most expensive car, the $3.9 million Lamborghini Veneno...

...and on and on. If you're unemployed with almost zero chance of ever getting any work, what are you meant to do? And again, just focussing on Europe, bear in mind that roughly 5% of the unemployed are Muslims.

With its promise of a guaranteed income plus free housing, food, clothing, health care and hospitals, ISIS is looking more attractive every day. Especially as, whatever else it is, and in sharp contrast with our increasingly rich-take-all Western societies, ISIS is profoundly egalitarian and democratic.

Note that there was a well-established precedent for this in pre-Islamic Arabia where tribes were always led by a democratically elected leader or *sheikh*, Arabic for old man, whose term lasted as long as he found favor with his followers.

So in spite of its barbarities and atrocities, we have to admit that in going back to the very founding of Islam, if nothing else, ISIS believes in equality.

On to another motivation: sex.

"I am raping you for God," said the ISIS fighter to the terrified twelve-year old girl.

As she struggled to break free of him, he explained that what he was doing was not a sin, indeed the Koran gave him the right to rape her because she was not a Muslim, she was an unbeliever, and by raping her he was drawing closer to God.

He bound her hands and gagged her, then he knelt beside the bed and prostrated himself in prayer before getting on top of her.

When it was over, he knelt to pray again.

Is this justified in the Koran? No. The Arabic word for "rape," *ghasab*, is never once used in the Holy Book.

So why is this man raping a 12-year old girl? He is doing it because she is a Kurdish Yazidi, whose ancient Zoroastrian religion ISIS considers to be devil-worshipping, enabling this monster to force her to have sex with him because she is a captive and a slave.

Slavery? Where did that come from in the 21st century?

Dates when slavery was abolished in key countries and empires:

1833: British Empire   1923: Afghanistan
1865: United States   1924: Iraq
1877: Egypt   1928: Iran
1882: Ottoman Empire   1952: Qatar
1886: Cuba   1962: Saudi Arabia
1888: Brazil   1962: Yemen
1906: China   1964: UAE
1922: Morocco   1970: Oman

2014: ISIS **restores** slavery

So the poor little 12-year old is a slave and our intrepid ISIS fighter can rape her to his heart's content.

There is even an ISIS "rape manual," arranged in a handy Q&A format that explains it all.

The cover reads:

> *Questions and Answers*
> *regarding*
> ## The Captive and the Slaves
> *Office of Research and Advice*

Question 4: Is it permissible to have intercourse with a female captive?

It is permissible to have sexual intercourse with the female captive. God the almighty said: '[Successful are the believers] who guard their chastity, except from their wives or [the captives and slaves] that their right hands possess, for then they are free from blame' [Koran 23:5-6]

ISIS interprets this well known Koranic verse, which boils down to "you don't need to guard your chastity with female slaves" to mean "go ahead and rape little girls." A nauseating mashup of piety and pedophilia.

On that subject, the following price list for both Yazidi and Christian slaves, which must be posted at all ISIS sales of sex slaves on pain of death:

Price List – Sale of Booty

We have been informed that the market for the sale of women has been experiencing a drop in price, which affects the needs of the Islamic State and the funding of the Mujahideen. Because of this, the Commerce Department has decided to set a series of fixed prices for the sale of women. All auctioneers are to abide by these prices and anyone who breaks the rules will be executed.

PRICE (in Iraqi dinars)	MERCHANDISE
200,000	age 1-9: Yazidi/Christian
150,000	age 10-20: Yazidi/Christian
100,000	age 21-30: Yazidi/Christian
75,000	age 31-40: Yazidi/Christian
50,000	age 41-50: Yazidi/Christian

[100,000 Iraqi dinars = $86 U.S.]

Limited to 3 Sex Slaves per person except
for foreign sales to Turks, Syrians and the Gulf States

Baby girls are worth a fortune, grandmothers go for a song.

In spite of the obscenity of this desecration of female bodies – the younger the better – there is no doubt that this is one of ISIS's top recruiting tools.

If ISIS is the perfect refuge for psychopaths, it also provides a very safe haven for pedophiles.

Psychopathy, religious mania, call of duty, black and white thinking, identity crises, racism, longing for acceptance, income inequality, pedophilia... all of these factors play a part in the formation of the ISIS mind and its attraction for so many people.

But there is also something much deeper going on. Something buried deep beneath the consciousness of the people drawn to ISIS – something buried beneath the consciousness of all of us.

We all have our own millennial dreams of the perfect world, our archetypal visions of some Nirvana where we will live happily ever after. In all of these dreams, the transcendent king of our lost days of glory will return to bring about our Heaven on Earth. This king has many names. Moses leading the Jewish people to the Promised Land...

Jesus dying for our sins and then returning to save us once and for all by defeating the Antichrist at Armageddon...

Muhammad reciting God's words and leading his followers to conquer the world for Islam, and all of them fighting to rid the planet of evil and pave the way for an earthly Paradise...

Literature is replete with stories of the return of the king, this hero's journey, from Ulysses setting sail on his long and treacherous trip back to his wife Penelope in Ithaca...

...to King Arthur and his Knights of the Round Table's quest for the Holy Grail...

All such tales tap into our collective unconscious, as does the current real-life story of the return of the ISIS king in the form of "the first true Caliph of Islam in a thousand years," Abu Bakr al-Baghdadi...

...as he leads his followers in establishing their own version of Heaven on Earth at the final apocalyptic showdown with "Rome," the Crusading Christian West, destined to take place at Dabiq.

We are not consciously aware that al-Baghdadi is the returning king of our dreams. But our subconscious is, simultaneously blinding the most impressionable among us to the horrors of ISIS and driving us to embark on its heroic journey.

Yet another motivation: the Arabic language itself.

Islam is Arabic and Arabic is Islam. You can't have one without the other. Whether your mother tongue is Kurdish, Turkish, Urdu, Malay, Filipino, Khazakh, Russian, Persian, Dari or Pashto – or English, German or French, for that matter – if you're a Muslim or a convert to Islam, you will find yourself using Arabic a great deal of the time.

Why is this? Simply because of this book, the Holy Koran:

All of today's 1.6 billion Muslims have to believe that the period between 610 and 632 when Muhammad received God's revelations represents the one and only period during which God spoke to man since the universe began. And of course God – via the angel Gabriel – spoke in Arabic.

This fact has enormous ramifications. The best way to illustrate this is to step into a literary time machine. All we have to do is start reading any passage of written Arabic to find ourselves traveling down that passage through time, all the way back to the Arabian desert in the early six hundreds.

It doesn't matter what we're reading, an Egyptian novel written last year or a recipe for bread pudding written this morning, it will be in exactly the same Arabic, letter for letter and dot for dot, that was used almost fourteen centuries ago. How much of our English language could we understand as it was written that long ago when bread pudding would have come out in Old English as *beorma rn-earhgehæcc*?

How did the Arabic language get stuck back in the seventh century?

The reason is quite simple. As we've said before, when God spoke to Muhammad in that cave via the Angel Gabriel, He of course spoke in the language of the desert dwellers of the day, so at that instant that particular desert dialect of Arabic suddenly froze, as solid and immutable as the Kaaba itself in Holy Mecca.

If the Jews are the Chosen People, Arabic is the Chosen Language.

As we've also said before, this is the basis of Islam itself, the foundation of the faith of every Muslim. Precisely because God only spoke to Muhammad, and precisely because He spoke in Arabic, all Muslims have to believe every word of the following sentence *in Arabic*:

لا إله إلا الله محمد رسول الله

lā 'ilāha 'illā-llāh, muḥammadun rasūlu-llāh
There is no god but God,
Muhammad is His Messenger

Just as they have to believe every word of a speech by an ISIS leader exhorting them to kill all the Shias, or enslave all the Yazidi women, or do almost anything to anyone else who doesn't toe the party line.

In any other language, you might have a chance to analyze the message, to criticize it. But in Arabic, it is irresistible stuff, by definition uncriticizable. For every word and phrase is the voice of God ringing down the centuries.

No wonder we are confounded by ISIS. If you don't know the language, it is impossible to understand what is really going on; you will never know what's happening in their heads. No translation can get close. It's not like going from German to English, or even from Hindi to English. It's like going from another galaxy to ours.

In every sense of the word, Arabic is a different script that tells a different story. And all because of that moment nearly 1,400 years ago that deified both its spoken and written form.

Final – and perhaps most deep-rooted – motivation of all for many Muslims to join ISIS: nostalgia.

To begin to understand this motivation, let's start with ISIS's promise of a glorious Islamic Caliphate spanning the globe.

Why is this concept so irresistible to so many Muslims? Because of their profound sense of nostalgia for the "Golden Age of Islam."

What was this Golden Age? To get an inkling, all you have to do is look up at the night sky.

If it is a very clear night, you'll probably be able to make out tens of thousands of stars with a regular telescope. Of these, a little over 300 have been named. About two-thirds of these names — 210 to be precise — come from one particular language. Which language do you think this is?

Arabic.

Now look at these words: *alchemy, alcove, algebra, algorithm, alkali, almanac*. Which language do you think they came from?

Arabic again. (The *al* means "the.") The very word we say at the end of Christian and Jewish prayers, Amen, comes from the Arabic for "I believe": *Ameen*.

When a Western woman gets up in the morning, she wraps herself in the language: *muslin* from Mosul, or *gauze* from Gaza or *damask* from Damascus or *satin* or *cotton* or *mohair*, perhaps colored *lilac* or *crimson* or covered in *sequins*.

So many Arabic words in the English language.

We even count the stars above our heads using Arabic numbers, including the concept of *zero* – another Islamic invention (and Arabic word).

	Arabic Numbers			
٠	٤	٣	٢	١
5	4	3	2	1
١٠	٩	٨	٧	٦
10	9	8	7	6

How was Arabic able to exert such influence over our own – and many other – European languages?

A quick history lesson. For centuries following the fall of Rome in 476 A.D., Western Europe was a benighted backwater, a pestilential, poverty-stricken world, bogged down in what are so aptly described as the "Dark Ages."

Meanwhile, the Islamic world was booming…

…especially in the magnificent city of Baghdad, which by 800 A.D. was the richest and largest city on earth.

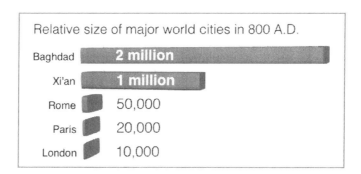

A magical land of Scheherazade weaving her 1001 stories to the great Caliph every Arabian Night…

...Aladdin... Ali Baba... Sinbad the Sailor...

Baghdad wasn't just the biggest, most magical city in the world, it also had the biggest library. At a time when the richest monasteries in Western Europe might have had 2 or 3 dozen books, Baghdad's "House of Wisdom" housed 400,000.

The Caliph paid an army of translators the equivalent of $24,000 a month to translate nothing less than the whole of human wisdom – from Ancient Greece and Rome, Persia, India and China – all into Arabic.

But these translators weren't only Arabs, any more than they were only Muslims. They were Jews and Christians, Persians and Kurds and Sunnis and Shias…

...all working together in the most tolerant empire the world had ever seen to save – and vastly enlarge and improve upon – the learning of the ancients for all mankind.

This is why our modern languages are saturated with Arabic and why many Muslims today look back on this period so fondly.

Until it all began to come crashing down when a series of calamitous events took place.

The first calamity was to last for exactly 200 years, from 1091-1291: when the Crusaders...

...came looting and pillaging and slaughtering their way across the Middle East, bent on retaking the Holy Land for Christianity – and grabbing as much of its wealth and culture and learning as they could.

Ultimately their conquest failed of course, but they succeeded in trashing large swathes of the Islamic world in the process.

However, the culminating calamity for Baghdad came not from the West, but from the East with the rampaging Mongol hordes of Hulagu Kahn...

...who utterly destroyed the city in 1258...

...butchering half its population and demolishing all its mosques, palaces, hospitals and libraries, including the great House of Wisdom itself.

The final two disasters to befall the Islamic Empire were brought about almost simultaneously near the end of the 1400s by two sailors.

Until that time, the Middle East had been the crossroads of the known world.

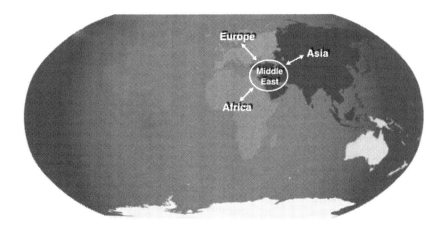

Christopher Columbus and Vasco da Gama changed all that when they bypassed the Middle East, making it a backwater in its turn.

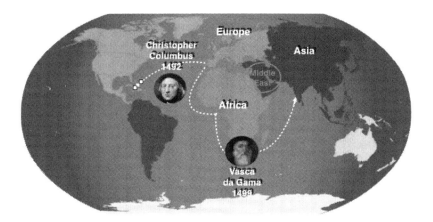

The region has never recovered its former glory. Hence the nostalgia on the part of many Muslims for their thousand-year old Golden Age and the desire of some of them to join ISIS.

Which of course is yet another irony, since everything ISIS stands for is the exact opposite of the Golden Age of Islam.

6. Why is ISIS so barbaric?

If the ISIS punishments alluded tod in chapter 3 weren't so monstrously cruel, they would almost be funny, compiled by a group of primitive cultists with apparently zero sense of humor and awareness of the absurd.

But the ISIS members are deadly serious about this. Why are they so barbaric? What basis do their draconian punishments have in Islam itself and in the Koran?

To answer that, let's just focus on ISIS's penal code of punishments for its own members which they published in January 2015:

> *One.* Blasphemy against God: Death.
> *Two.* Blasphemy against the Prophet Muhammad: Death – even if the accuser repents.
> *Three.* Blasphemy against Islam: Death.
> *Four.* Adultery: Stoning until death in case the adulterer was married and 100 lashes and exile if he or she was unmarried.
> *Five.* Sodomy: Death for the person committing the act, as well as for the one receiving it.
> *Six.* Theft: Cutting off the hand.
> *Seven.* Drinking alcohol: 80 lashes.
> *Eight.* Slandering: 80 lashes.
> *Nine.* Spying for the unbelievers: Death by Crucifixion.
> *Ten.* Apostasy: Death by Crucifixion.

Now let's go though these ten punishments, checking what the Koran has to say about each one, starting with the original Arabic and translating it into English. The first three punishments can be chunked into one under the heading of blasphemy.

One. Blasphemy against God: Death.

Two. Blasphemy against the Prophet Muhammad: Death – even if the accuser repents.

Three. Blasphemy against Islam: Death.

What does the Koran say about these three punishments? Actually, nothing at all directly. The Arabic word for blasphemy, تجديف *tajdeef*, appears nowhere in the Koran. There is only one verse that could possibly be construed as having anything to do with "blaspheming" God and the Prophet and Islam, and that is Chapter 33, Verse 57:

إِنَّ الَّذِينَ يُؤْذُونَ اللَّهَ وَرَسُولَهُ لَعَنَهُمُ اللَّهُ فِي الدُّنْيَا وَالْآخِرَةِ وَأَعَدَّ لَهُمْ عَذَابًا مُهِينًا

This transliterates as: ʾinna lladhīna yuʾdhūna llāha wa-rasūlahū laʿanahumu llāhu fī d-dunyā wa-l-ʾākhirati wa-ʾaʿadda lahum ʿadhāban muhīnan.

"Verily, those who harm God and His Messenger, God has cursed them in this world and the Hereafter and has prepared for them a humiliating torment."

You can't get much vaguer than that, and it has nothing to do with blaspheming in any sense of the word, let alone decapitating those who harmed God or His Messenger, or doing anything to them in this world other than cursing them. As for blaspheming Islam (meaning submission to God), the word "Islam" is never once used in the Koran as a title for the religion of the Muslims.

That use of the word didn't come into common parlance until after the death of Muhammad in 632 A.D. The closest the Koran gets to saying that the name of the new religion is Islam is the following:

إنَّ الدّينَ عِندَ اللهَ الإِسلامُ

ʾinna d-dīna ʿinda llāhi l-ʾislāmu
"Verily, with God religion is submission."

Four. Adultery: Stoning until death in case the adulterer was married and 100 lashes and exile if he or she were unmarried.

Koran, Chapter 24, Verse 2:

الزَّانِيَةُ وَالزَّاني فَاجلِدوا كُلَّ واحِدٍ مِنهُما مِائَةَ جَلدَةٍ وَلا تَأخُذكُم بِهِما رَأفَةٌ في دينِ اللهِ إِن كُنتُم تُؤمِنونَ بِاللهِ وَاليَومِ الآخِرِ وَليَشهَد عَذابَهُما طائِفَةٌ مِنَ المُؤمِنينَ

'az-zāniyatu wa-z-zānī fa-jlidū kulla wāḥidin minhumā mi'ata jaldatin wa-lā ta'khudhkum bihimā ra'fatun fī dīni llāhi 'in kuntum tu'minūna bi-llāhi wa-l-yawmi l-'ākhiri wa-l-yashhad 'adhābahumā ṭā'ifatun mina l-mu'minīna

"As for the fornicatress and the fornicator, whip each of them with a hundred lashes, and let no pity for them overcome you if you believe in God and the Last Day, and let their punishment be witnessed by a group of the faithful."

The Arabic words *'az-zāniyatu wa-z-zānī* are ambiguous: they can either mean the fornicatress and the fornicator or the adulteress and the adulterer. In either case, stoning doesn't come into it. In fact, the Arabic word for stoning, رجم *rajam* appears nowhere in the Koran.

Five. Sodomy: Death for the person committing the act, as well as for the one receiving it.

The Arabic for sodomy, لواط *liwat*, does not appear once in the Koran. The only text that could possibly be construed as referring to sodomy is in Chapter 4, Verse 16:

وَاللَّذَانِ يَأْتِيَانِهَا مِنكُمْ فَآذُوهُمَا ۖ فَإِن تَابَا وَأَصْلَحَا فَأَعْرِضُوا عَنْهُمَا ۗ إِنَّ اللَّهَ كَانَ تَوَّابًا رَحِيمًا

wa-lladhāni ya'tiyānihā minkum fa-'ādhūhumā fa-'in tābā wa-'aṣlaḥā fa-'a'riḍū 'anhumā 'inna llāha kāna tawwāban raḥīman

"And the two of you who commit it, inflict pain on them both; but if they repent and reform, turn way from them. Verily, God is merciful and compassionate."

This verse manages to be simultaneously obscure, ambiguous, vague and contradictory: "commit" what? We have no idea. And the "two of you": A man and a woman? Two men? Two women? But let's assume we're talking about two men and they have committed "it," i.e. sodomy, the hazy punishment of "inflicting pain on them" is a long way from executing them – or pushing them off tall buildings, as ISIS is wont to do. And even if we do inflict pain on them, if they "repent and reform," we should "turn away" from them because "God is merciful and compassionate."

Six. Theft: Cutting off the hand.

وَالسَّارِقُ وَالسَّارِقَةُ فَاقْطَعُوا أَيْدِيَهُما جَزَاءً بِما كَسَبا نَكَالًا مِنَ اللَّهَ وَاللَّهُ عَزِيزٌ حَكِيمٌ

wa-s-sāriqu wa-s-sāriqatu fa-qta'ū 'aydiyahumā jazā'an bi-mā kasabā nakālan mina llāhi wa-llāhu 'azīzun ḥakīmun

"As for the thief, man or woman, cut off their hands according to what they have gained, as an exemplary punishment from God, and God is all-mighty, all-wise."

This is the *only* item on ISIS's list of punishments that is justified by a verse in the Koran – although even here the "according to" is ambiguous. Does this mean that if you gain very little from your theft you will spared amputation? Or that only one hand will be cut off?

Note that cutting off thieves' hands in medieval times was a standard punishment throughout Europe continuing through most of the 1700s, but that is of course no excuse for Muslims doing it today.

Seven. Drinking alcohol: 80 lashes.

There is no punishment in the Koran for drinking alcohol – certainly not lashing. The only specific statement about this is 4:43:

أَيُّهَا الَّذِينَ آمَنوا لا تَقرَبُوا الصَّلاةَ وَأَنتُم سُكارىٰ حَتّىٰ تَعلَموا ما تَقولونَ

yā-ʾayyuhā lladhīna ʾāmanū lā taqrabū ṣ-ṣalāta wa-ʾantum sukārā ḥattā taʿlamū mā taqūlūna.

"O you who have faith! Do not approach prayer when you are intoxicated until you know what you are saying."

Eight. Slandering: 80 lashes.

The word for slander الافتراء *iftira'* does not appear in the Koran, nor is there a punishment specified for it.

Nine. Spying for the unbelievers: Death by Crucifixion.

Koran, 49:12

يَا أَيُّهَا الَّذِينَ آمَنُوا اجْتَنِبُوا كَثِيرًا مِنَ الظَّنِّ إِنَّ بَعْضَ الظَّنِّ إِثْمٌ وَلَا تَجَسَّسُوا وَلَا يَغْتَب بَعْضُكُم بَعْضًا

yā-'ayyuhā lladhīna 'āmanū jtanibū kathīran mina z-zanni 'inna ba'da z-zanni 'ithmun wa-lā tajassasū wa-lā yaghtab ba'dukum ba'dan.

"O you who have faith! Avoid much suspicion. Indeed some suspicions are sins. And do not spy on or backbite one another."

So the Koran frowns upon spying, تجسس. tajassus. It can even be a sin. But not a word about punishment – not to speak of crucifixion.

Ten. Apostasy: Death by Crucifixion.

There are many references in the Koran to apostasy (renunciation of what is to become the Islamic faith), ردة or *riddah* in Arabic, but not a single mention of an earthly punishment for apostasy, and certainly no mention of crucifixion. In fact, the only mention of crucifixion at all in the Holy Book is as one of the punishments for banditry. and causing "corruption on the earth."

Here are extracts from the two Koranic verses that most Islamic scholars maintain settle the matter of apostasy and its supposed punishment once and for all:

Koran, 2:256:

لا إكراهَ فِي الدّينِ

lā ʾikrāha fī d-dīni
"There is no compulsion in religion."

Koran, 18:29:

فَمَن شاءَ فَلْيُؤْمِن وَمَن شاءَ فَلْيَكْفُر

fa-man shāʾa fa-l-yuʾmin wa-man shāʾa fa-l-yakfur
"Let him who wishes believe and let him who wishes disbelieve."

So, with the sole exception of theft, ISIS has zero Koranic justification for its barbaric list of punishments.

Where does the so-called "Islamic State" get this stuff from then?

Well, first of all from Wahhabism, as we've noted, which is to say in today's world from Saudi Arabia, whose crime and punishment list is virtually identical to the ISIS one.

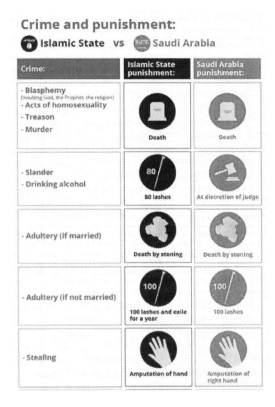

ISIS's second source of wisdom about Islamic crime and punishment comes from the Hadith…

...a voluminous collection of literally hundreds of thousands of anecdotes about the supposed sayings and doings of the Prophet Muhammad passed on from Islamic scholar to Islamic scholar, most of them dating from at least 200 years after his death. Not surprisingly, just as in the game of "Chinese Whispers"...

...by the time the anecdote reaches the end of the he said-she said-he-said-she said chain it has often become something else entirely. The upshot of this being that many of the Hadith are so varied and contradictory – not only between themselves and the Koran, but also between each other – you can find prophetic justification for just about anything you want in them – including the aforementioned list of brutal medieval punishments.

To complicate things yet further, many of these brutal Hadith have become the basis of Islamic Law, otherwise known as Sharia.

Does this mean that in all Islamic countries where Sharia law obtains – which in varying degrees is almost all of them – they slice blasphemers' heads off and push homosexuals off tall buildings in true ISIS fashion?

Not at all. We said "where Sharia law obtains in *varying degrees,*" and these degrees vary enormously. For example, out of the 50 countries with a Muslim majority, only six have the death penalty for blasphemy or apostasy: Afghanistan, Pakistan, Iran, Abu Dhabi, Dubai (the two leading emirates in the United Arab Emirates) and Saudi Arabia.

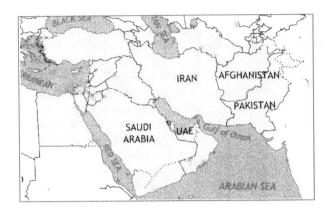

And with the sole exception of Saudi Arabia, these penalties are rarely applied.

Crowds gather for a beheading in Riyadh's "Chop Chop" Square

So to sum up: there is almost no justification in the Koran for ISIS's appalling punishments. Why does ISIS keep doing these terrible things then? The answer can be summed up in three words: *reign of terror*.

In the previous chapter, we talked of the possible role of psychopathy in the ISIS fighter's mental makeup, of an element of madness in the organization. But if this is madness, there is a great deal of method to it.

First and foremost, ISIS doesn't go around cutting people's heads off just for fun, or simply because they're bloodthirsty ghouls. They do it to intimidate. It is in fact a very carefully orchestrated and precisely planned reign of terror.

Sound familiar? When was the last time we heard of a "reign of terror"? The French Revolution. And what was those revolutionaries' favorite occupation? Cutting people's heads off.

The amputation of heads is in fact a favorite strategy of apocalyptic movements, from the "Thousand-Year Reich" of the Nazis...

...to the Cultural Revolution of Mao Zedong...

ISIS terror is a systematically applied policy that even has its own manual: *The Management of Savagery*, by al-Qaeda writer, Abu Bakr Naji.

"We are preparing for another wave of operations which will fill their hearts with fear and this fear will have no end... the most abominable savagery is still preferable than stability under the order of the unbelievers... the Crusader/Zionist enemy."

Just as in the case of the French revolutionaries, the Nazis and Mao Zedong, and many other cataclysmic forces from the Mongol hordes...

...to Khmer Rouge...

...the goal is always to scare you into submission.

Far from apologizing for its inhumanity, ISIS floods the world's media with gory images and videos and descriptions of its barbarity, taunting the world with it, stunning us with horror, and going to great lengths to confirm that the acts that horrify us are not the work of rogue members but are, indeed, the organization's official policy of psychological warfare.

[The Arabic reads: "This man waged war on Muslims and detonated an explosive here."]

The subtitle of Abu Bakr an-Naji's savagery manual is "A report on the stage through which the *Umma* is passing."

Umma meaning the nation or country – or state, in this instance, for, as we've seen, that is what the first "IS" in ISIS stands for: the Islamic State.

7. Islam and ISIS Women

Are all the ISIS fighters and supporters men? No, in fact about 10% of them are women, who like their male counterparts, come mainly from the Middle East, but also from many foreign countries all over the world.

Why are all these women shrouded from head to foot in burkas? Where is it written in the Koran that they should dress in this ridiculous fashion? Nowhere. In fact, almost the only mention of any sort of covering at all for women in the 600-odd pages of the Holy Book is in Chapter 24, Verse 31:

> And say to the believing women, that they cast down their eyes and **guard their private parts**, and reveal not their adornment save such as is outward; and let them cast their veils over their **bosoms**, and not reveal their adornment save to their husbands, or their fathers, or their husbands' fathers, or their sons, or their husbands' sons, or their brothers, or their brothers' sons...

In other words, don't go out in public topless and bottomless. An edict that is obeyed even on the licentious streets of the Godless Western World last time we checked.

But not all women who join ISIS are lucky enough to be chosen as fighters. The great majority are simply "wives."

Tragically, we already know the fate of these unlucky wives. They lead isolated lives spent mostly indoors without electricity or clean water. They wear heavy head-face-and-body covering in 100 degree weather and they are humiliated, harassed, and punished if their burqa slips.

Basically, all they are allowed to do is cook, clean, sew, have sex, produce babies, and pray. They are in fact nothing more than an assembly line set up to pleasure male fighters and provide them with offspring. When their (arranged marriage) husbands are killed in battle, they are expected to celebrate their "martyrdom" and immediately marry other fighters.

The sex slaves of course lead an even more hellish life. These mainly Yazidi and Christian girls and women are raped up to thirty times a day by different men and forced to perform pornographic acts that terrify and injure them. Many attempt suicide. Many are sold – over and over again – or trafficked to Saudi Arabia or North Africa.

This brave fighter is announcing his marriage to a terrified seven-year old girl, permitted by Islam according to ISIS because she is an "unbeliever."

Is this "Islamic" behavior? It couldn't be less so. Historically, Muslim women have been far more powerful than their non-Muslim equivalents in the Western World.

Let's start with four examples, two from the earliest days of Islam, a third from its Golden Age, and a fourth from Muslim India. We'll begin with Khadija bint Khuwaylid, who was a very successful trader in Mecca with many "agents" representing her on her caravans.

In 595, when Khadija was 40, it came to her notice that one of these agents, a 25-year old man by the name of Muhammad, was said to be the expected Prophet. She proposed marriage to him, and they had six children together. Khadija is commonly regarded as the "Mother of the Believers," and was the first person of either sex to convert to Islam.

Our second example of a highly successful and respected Muslim woman is Nusaybah bint Ka'ab, who was also a very early convert to Islam, renowned for shielding the Prophet from the arrows of the enemy in one of his early battles where she was severely wounded herself.

Still from the Middle East
Broadcasting Center's TV series

Next, a word about Lubna of Cordoba (d. 984), palace secretary in the Umayyad palace in Cordoba. She was also a skilled mathematician and a poet, who excelled in writing and grammar and presided over the royal library, which consisted of over 500,000 books.

(Painting of Lubna by José Luis Muñoz)

Finally, we come to Razia Sultan, who was the ruler of the Sultanate of Delhi between 1236 and 1240.

Razia was a major patron of learning, establishing schools and libraries across northern India. In all matters, she behaved like a sultan, leading armies and sitting upon the throne

Now for some recent examples of powerful Muslim women.

The contrast between ISIS and most of the modern Islamic world could hardly be greater.

To illustrate this, a question: out of the 44 presidents and 47 vice-presidents of the United States, how many have been women?

Zero.

Out of all the Islamic countries in the world, how many presidents, vice-presidents or prime ministers have been women?

Count them:

Tanzu Giller, PM of Turkey

Benazir Bhutto, PM of Pakistan

Mame Madior Boye PM of Senegal

Megawati Sukarnoputri, PM of Indonesia

Bibi Ameena Firadaus, President of Mauritius
Rosa Otunbayeva, PM of Kyrgyzstan
Atifeta Jahjaga, PM of Kosovo
Sheikh Hasina Wajed, PM ofBangladesh
Khaleda Zia, PM of Bangladesh
Gissé Mariam Kaidama Sidibé, President of Mali
Masoumeh Ebtekar, Vice-President of Iran

Total of Islamic female presidents, vice-presidents or prime ministers: eleven.

2nd question: 19% of the seats in the US Congress are held by women. How many majority Muslim countries have a higher percentage of seats held by women in their parliaments than the US?

Count these too:

% of parliament seats held by women

1. Senegal 43%
2. Algeria 32%
3. Tunisia 31%
4. Egypt 30%
5. Afghanistan 28%
6. Turkmenistan 26%
7. Iraq 25%
8. Kazakhstan 25%
9. Sudan 24%
10. Kyrgyzstan 23%
11. Uzbekistan 22%
12. Guinea 22%
13. Pakistan 21%
14. Albania 20%
15. UAE 18%
16. Malawi 17%
17. Indonesia 17%
18. Morocco 17%
19. Somalia 14%
20. Turkey 14%
21. Niger 13%
22. Djbouti 13%
23. Jordan 12%
24. Syria 12%
25. Malaysia 10%
26. Mali 10%
27. Gambia 9%
28. Bahrain 8%
29. Maldives 6%
30. Lebanon 3%
31. Iran 3%
32. Kuwait 2%
33. Oman 0%
34. Qatar 0%
35. Saudi Arabia 0%
36. Yemen 0%

So in many Islamic countries women are faring remarkably well – better in 14 cases than in the United States itself.

But now for a 3rd and final question: Who is the most famous teenage girl on earth? It is important you learn the answer to this question because it simultaneously illustrates what is right and what is wrong with the Islamic world where females are concerned.

Before we give you the answer, let us put you in this Muslim teenager's shoes for a moment. You are fifteen years old and it is the end of the school day. You make your way to the bus waiting outside the gates. You climb on board and sit beside one of your school friends. As the bus drives off, you notice that the usually busy road is deserted today.

You turn to your friend, "Why is there no one here? Can you see it's not the way it usually is?"

A few moments later, the bus is flagged down by two young men as it passes a clearing, only a hundred yards from the school gates.

"I've never seen them before," you say to your friend, as the two young men enter the bus.

She replies that they look like college students.

Then one of the young men asks the students on the bus, which one of them is you.

Your friend glances at you, innocently given you away, and the young man pulls out a pistol and fires three shots at your face. One bullet hits the left side of your forehead, travels under your skin through the length of your face, and then goes into your shoulder.

You remain in a coma for a week and are not expected to survive.

But you do.

Who are you in this true story? More clues. Here's the "school bus" you were traveling in when you were shot, nothing more than a covered pickup truck, open at the back, with three lines of benches running the length of the flatbed...

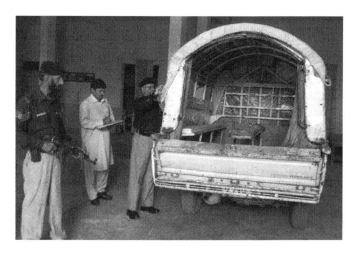

Here's the bench you were sitting on, covered in your blood...

Here you are being taken to the hospital...

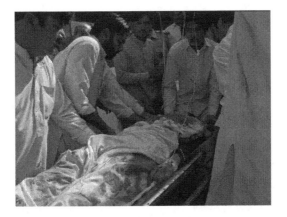

Here's one of thousands of candlelight vigils held for you around the world...

And then, miraculously, here you are addressing the United Nations, chatting with the Obamas, meeting the Queen, winning the Nobel Prize...

The "you" in question is of course Malala Yousafzai, now a world-famous Pakistani activist for female education and the world's youngest-ever Nobel Prize laureate.

It all began in 2009, when Malala was 11 and started to write an illustrated blog for the BBC describing life under the Taliban occupation of her beautiful Swat Valley and their attempts to control her "paradise" and ban girls from going to school.

Gradually, through her blog, Malala became better and better known, giving interviews for newspapers and on television, exposing the horrors the Taliban were inflicting on the Valley – including multiple threats aimed at her and her father.

Finally, to shut her down once and for all, on the afternoon of 9 October 2012, a Taliban gunman shot her in the face.

But the assassination attempt backfired and sparked a national and international outpouring of support for Malala.

The United Nations Special Envoy for Global Education Gordon Brown, former Prime Minister of the UK...

...demanded in Malala's name that all children worldwide be in school by the end of 2015. This was to lead to the ratification of Pakistan's first Right to Free and Compulsory Education Bill for all girls and boys.

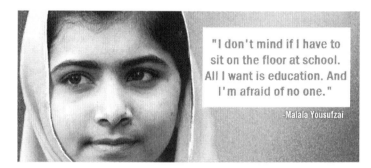

Thus did the writings of a little eleven-year old Muslim girl undo the mighty Taliban and show just how absurdly – and tragically – out of step they and al-Qaeda and ISIS and all the rest of the so-called "Islamic" terror groups are with the true Islam.

8. The growing threat of ISIS

The "Islamic State" taking over the world? How is this project going? The good news is that, as of May, 2016, thanks to intensified attacks by the US and its allies, ISIS had lost 45% of the territory it once held in Iraq and 20% of the areas it controlled in Syria.

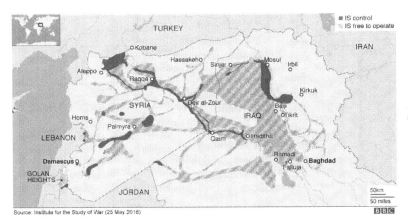

Air strikes in Iraq and Syria

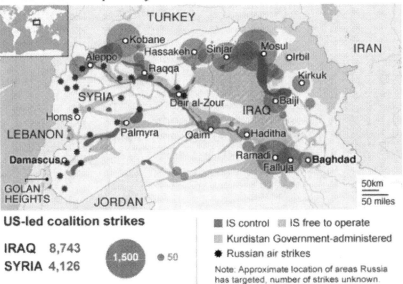

The much, much worse news is that like a virulent cancer, ISIS has compensated for these territorial losses by metastasizing to many parts of the globe. Small home-grown cells and lone wolf operatives "inspired" and/or directed by ISIS have popped up like malignant pustules from Africa and Asia to the US and Canada, wreaking havoc and killing many hundreds of innocent people tacks on Tunisia, Egypt, Paris, Brussels, San Bernardino, Orlando, Istanbul, Bangladesh, Baghdad, Nice…

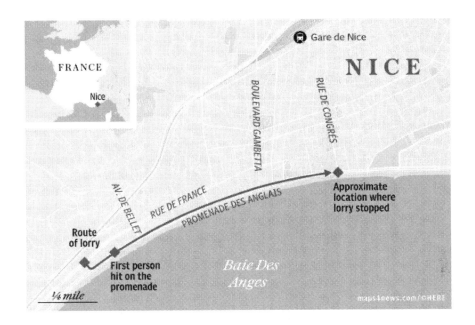

But although ISIS is going viral with a vengeance having lost so much ground in Iraq and Syria in recent months, it still has a very sophisticated government apparatus.

As a reminder, ISIS was formed in April 2013. Only a little over two years later, the Islamic State encompassed an area bigger than Great Britain...

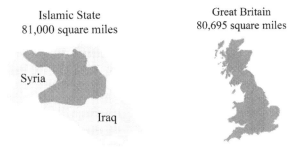

...covering almost half of Syria and at least one-third of Iraq, with a government similar in its organization to almost any other modern one.

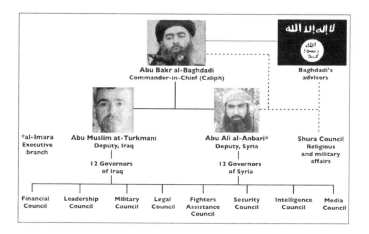

How did the so-called Islamic State manage to expand so fast and set up a government so rapidly, ruling over 6 million people? Or is their organization chart just a paper pipe dream?

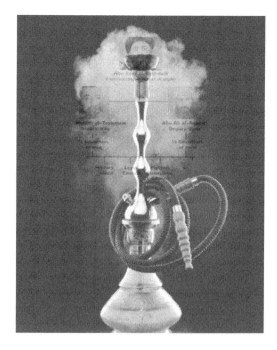

By no means. This is a fully functioning, real life government. It mints its own money: silver and gold dinars of "the First Caliphate." Here is the gold five-dinar coin (dated 1436, the Islamic equivalent of 2015)...

...with the map of the world on the back confirming that this will become the world's first global currency as announced in a number of ISIS movies and videos.

Throughout the territory it has conquered, which includes such formerly Iraqi cities as Mosul (population 1.5 million) and formerly Syrian cities, Raqqa (220,000), Tadmur (140,000), al-Bab (67,000) and al-Qaryatayn (14,000), the Islamic State has also opened its own banks...

...which do not of course charge interest. For once, ISIS does have a Koranic verse to justify what it does, since usury is indeed *haram* (forbidden) in the Koran, 2:275:

"Those who devour usury shall not rise again except as he rises, whom Satan of the touch prostrates; that is because they say, 'Trafficking (trade) is like usury.' God has permitted trafficking, and forbidden usury."

In Mosul, The State's banking system got a kick start from their looting...

...about half a billion dollars from that city's banks.

The State has its own police force, seen here guarding a police station (although crime is supposedly "non-existent" under ISIS)...

...directing traffic...

...and driving a freshly-painted police car.

The State also has its own law courts...

In addition, "Schools of Jihad" are spreading everywhere throughout the Islamic State...

...indoctrinating young children into the ISIS system of cruelty and violence...

Free healthcare is available to everyone in the Caliphate, reputedly modeled after Britain's National Health Service.

According to the Islamic State's online *Dabiq* magazine, their health system includes an extensive network of hospitals, clinics, pharmacies and medical colleges, all under the supervision of an Islamic State Health Council.

Here are the one-month combined statistics from two of the hospitals – again, courtesy *Dabiq* magazine.

Category	Amount
Outpatients	6711
Emergency Patients	4289
Lab Tests	15688
Minor X-Rays	2384
Kidney Dialysis Sessions	442
Physiotherapy Sessions	233
Children Admitted	170
Blood Donors	1151
General Surgeries	140
Bone Surgeries	261
Urinary Surgeries	18
Nerve Surgeries	15
Ear Surgeries	3
Gynecological Surgeries	47
Emergency Surgeries	16
Births	576
Audiometric Tests	45
Brain Stem Scans	11
Ultrasound Exams	400

On top of all this, in addition to *Dabiq*...

...as we mentioned in chapter 4, the Islamic State also has its own radio network, a*l-Bayan*, based in Mosul...

...its own satellite TV, *Tawheed*, based in Libya, and has announced its own forthcoming TV network: the Islamic Caliphate Broadcast...

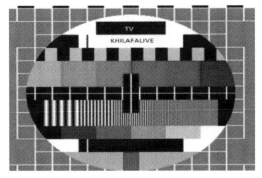

All this, under the aegis of ISIS'a *al-Hayat* Media Center…

And last but not least the Islamic State has of course its own army, which boasts about 6,400 tanks and other armored vehicles…

Not to mention the State's zero fear of any "Crusader" armies who might dare to oppose them, notably the Americans, whom the author of "The Management of Savagery," Abu Bakr Naji, summarily dismissed as having "reached a stage of effeminacy that made them incapable of sustaining battles for a long period of time."

Islam vs. ISIS

In chapter 4 we looked briefly at ISIS propaganda and their ingenious use of print, audio, video, film and social media. But it goes much deeper than that. In every sense of the word, as we'll see shortly.

But first of all a question: What do almost all ISIS fighters have in common? They are above all, *young*: in their late teens or early twenties...

And where do most young people spend most of their lives? Online. They were born into the Internet and are completely at home in it.

These youngsters were most likely recruited online in the first place, and once working with ISIS will certainly continue to spend a great deal of their time bent over computer screens, doing everything from generating a constant stream of recruiting blogs and RSS feeds about ISIS's battle triumphs and their glorious life in the Islamic State to hacking into Western retail sites to steal credit card details...

...or penetrating the database of the Pentagon's Twitter and YouTube accounts to access the emails, passwords, phone numbers and home addresses of retired U.S. army generals.

But the Islamic State's pubescent IT specialists and computer programmers do more than trawl for victims on the surface of the Web, they dive deep down to a whole other submarine world known as the "Deep Web," which is 500 times larger than the shallow "Surface Web" most of the rest of us are familiar with.

Here, deep down near the bottom of the information ocean, beyond the reach of conventional search engines, ISIS cybernauts can conduct their clandestine business and clinch their diabolical deals to their heart's content, with no fear of detection.

And this includes all their numerous illegal financial transac-

tions, which are made all the more secure when combined with a second cyber revolution: bitcoins, aka cryptocurrency.

Bitcoins are virtual money you can use to buy and sell things just like regular money, only "off the grid," without going through banks or credit card companies. Each bitcoin consists of a unique set of numbers, which can't be copied.

You can buy bitcoins with regular money from websites such as Coinbase...

...and then store them in your virtual "wallet"...

One of the big advantages of bitcoins is that all your transactions are as anonymous as the Deep Web itself: they can never be traced. All very neat and convenient for shopping, but also very neat and convenient for criminals, cocaine pushers, hardcore porn purveyors and terrorists who want to keep their dealings secret.

Which is just the way ISIS likes it.

Now a word about the ISIS "Caliph" himself.

On June 29, 2014, ISIS announced (in Arabic, English, German, French and Russian) the reestablishment of the caliphate, with Abu Bakr al-Baghdadi as Caliph…

…along with its new name for itself: "The Islamic State."

In the statement, ISIS claimed that it had fulfilled all the legal requirements for the caliphate and that all existing jihadi groups and indeed all Muslims around the world were religiously obligated to swear loyalty to the new Caliph Abu Bakr al-Baghdadi.

"All Muslims around the world" most emphatically did not agree, with The International Union of Muslim Scholars...

...led by influential Sunni cleric Dr Yusuf Al-Qaradawi...

...declaring unequivocally that, "Linking the concept of caliphate to an organization known to be extremist does *not* serve Islam... This caliphate concept is of *extreme importance* for all Muslims and requires consensus among Muslims worldwide."

Zero reaction from al-Baghdadi.

Who is this guy?

He was born (in 1971) Ibrahim Ali al-Badri as-Samarrai, before changing his name to that of Islam's first caliph, Abu Bakr...

...tacking on the nom de guerre al-Baghdadi.

There is a confusing hodgepodge of back stories associated with him, including the rumor that he was an Islamic scholar with various advanced degrees from various Baghdad universities. But until this day he has been so reclusive that he is nicknamed "the invisible sheikh," even wearing a mask when he addresses his commanders. His only public appearance has been on a video of a sermon he delivered in Mosul after ISIS took the city in June, 2014...

...the same video that we – and everybody else – have been reduced to use stills from over and over again for want of anything else.

The only other authenticated photos of Baghdadi are these two...

...plus this mug shot taken in 2004 when the U.S. arrested him on suspicion of being involved with a militant Sunni group...

...and held him at Camp Bucca...

This is the U.S. Army detention center in Iraq, which ironically enough turned out to be a training ground and networking opportunity for a whole host of jihadists, some of them writing down each other's cell phone numbers on the white elastic of their boxer shorts for later use when they got out.

"Boxers helped us win the war," as one former inmate of Camp Bucca was to quip.

A hot night in Bucca

In October 2011, because of a number of Baghdadi exploits involving al-Qaeda in Iraq, including several suicide bombings, the US officially designated him a "terrorist," offering a $10 million reward for information leading to his capture or death.

Apart from proclaiming himself Caliph of the Islamic State, Baghadi's only other authenticated claim to fame is kidnapping and repeatedly raping – along with four teenage Yazidi sex slaves – 25-year old Kayla Mueller from Prescott, Arizona…

...who had been working at the Spanish Médecins Sans Frontières hospital in Aleppo, Syria, where she was learning to speak Arabic.

One of the Yazidi girls who escaped from Baghdadi's clutches recently told the BBC that Kayla Mueller was later murdered by the Islamic State "because she was American."

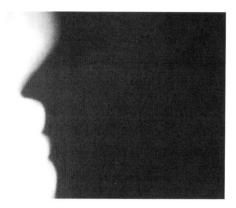

Well done, Baghdadi: fine qualifications for becoming leader of 1.6 billion Muslims across the globe.

9. Other Islamic terror organizations

So far in this book, we've concentrated on ISIS itself, but there are of course a number of other Islamic terror groups at large, some of whom are quasi-partners of the Islamic State, making it even more dangerous.

Here's the list of the eight other most important terrorist groups:

(i) Muslim Brotherhood
(ii) Hezbollah
(iii) Hamas
(iv) Taliban
(v) Boko Haram
(vi) Ash-Shabaab
(vii) Quds Force
(viii) An-Nusra Front

Before we begin, a note about languages. Until now, we've spoken almost exclusively about the Arabic-speaking parts of the Middle East and Africa.

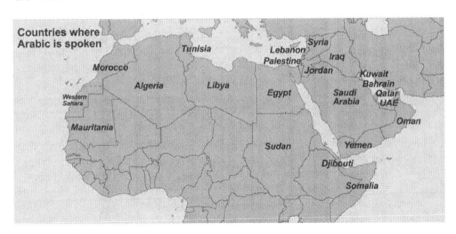

But some of the other Islamic terrorist groups on our list come from non-Arabic-speaking countries: Iran, Afghanistan, Pakistan,

Nigeria and Somalia, where a number of different languages are spoken.

Group	Country	Language(s)	Sect	Founded
Muslim Brotherhood	Egypt	Arabic	Sunni	1928
Hezbollah	Iran/Lebanon	Persian/Arabic	Shia	1982
Hamas	Gaza	Arabic	Sunni	1988
Taliban	Afghanistan/Pakistan	Pashto/Dari/Urdu	Sunni	1996
Boko Haram	Nigeria	Hausa	Sunni	2002
Ash-Shabab	Somalia	Somali/Arabic	Sunni	2006
Quds Force	Iran	Persian	Shia	2007
An-Nusra Front	Syria	Arabic	Sunni	2012

(i) Muslim Brotherhood

After Wahhabism, which we discussed in chapter 2, the next major Islamic revival came – predictably enough – hard on the heels of World War One, fueled by a toxic mix of anger, resentment and grievance on the part of some Muslims at what the West had inflicted on on them, both militarily and culturally.

The reaction of these Muslims, just like ibn al-Wahhab before them, was to create a rigid ideology based on the traditional values and laws of the Koran: what we know today as Islamic Fundamentalism, Radical Islam or simply Islamism.

Islamism was – and remains – a struggle to return to the glorious days when Islam reigned supreme, a yearning for the "pure" Islam practiced by the prophet. Not unlike the American Amish…

...the movement rejected much that was innovative. But the Islamists took the rejection of modernity a step further. They perceived those who had introduced these innovations, i.e. the West, to be their deadly enemy.

This first modern Islamist movement came to a head in 1928 with the founding of The Society of the Muslim Brothers (Arabic: جماعة الإخوان المسلمين), shortened to the Muslim Brotherhood الإخوان المسلمون *al-Ikhwān al-Muslimūn,* literally, The Muslim Brothers, which sounds like a singing group.

Even more incongruously, the motto on their logo, وَأَعِدُّوا *wa a'iddu,* "And prepare"...

...might have been lifted from Baden-Powell's 1907 motto "Be prepared."

Ironically, as it turned out, the Brotherhood actually do look like a bit like Boy Scouts when compared with their repulsive 21st century offspring, al-Qaeda and ISIS. Violent as many of the Brotherhood's activities have been, they don't go around decapitating people and raping small children.

The Muslim Brotherhood was founded in Egypt by Islamic scholar and schoolteacher Hassan al-Banna...

...the grandfather of Islamism's and ISIS's harshest critic, Oxford professor, Tariq Ramadan, as noted in chapter 2...

The Brotherhood was soon to develop armed cells that attacked the government and its supporters. Not surprisingly, the movement was outlawed and al-Banna was executed in Cairo in 1949.

But this didn't stop the Brotherhood's Islamism from continuing to grow, inspired in the 1950s by the jihadist writings of the Egyptian Sayyid Qutb...

In 1966, Qutb was convicted of plotting to assassinate Egyptian president Gamal Abdul Nasser...

...and was executed by hanging.

But in addition to preaching an extreme form of Islamism, the Brotherhood has been a benevolent social movement, teaching the illiterate and setting up business enterprises and hospitals…

After the overthrow of the Egyptian President Mubarak in 2011…

...the Muslim Brotherhood was legalized and in 2012, one of its leading members, Mohamed Morsi...

...became Egypt's first democratically elected president.

One year later, following massive demonstrations protesting repressive religious policies, Morsi was overthrown by the military and replaced in 2014 by the Commander-in-Chief of the Egyptian Armed Forces, Abdel Fattah el-Sisi…

…with the enthusiastic support of the US…

…as he set about imprisoning tens of thousands of dissidents and murdering thousands more…

...proving himself to be an even more brutal dictator than Mubarak...

As for Morsi, he rails in vain in his soundproof prison cage...

To sum up: the Muslim Brotherhood and ISIS are radically different. The Brotherhood's position is one of democracy, pluralism, reform, and integration, while ISIS is all about brutality, coercion, annihilation and despotism.

It seems highly unlikely that ISIS will ever get any support from the Brotherhood – or that ISIS would ever seek such support.

(ii) Hezbollah

Hezbollah, the Persian (i.e., Iranian) version of the Arabic for "Party of God" is third oldest Islamic terrorist group.

Hezbollah's green-on-yellow flag tells us a lot about the organization:

The logo makes it plain that Hezbollah equates God with War by showing a stylized representation of the Arabic words حـزب الله (*hizbu-llāh*)" with the first vertical letter of...

...reaching up to grasp an assault rifle (Arabic is written from right to left). The text above the logo reads in Arabic فـإن حـزب الله هـم

الـــغـالـــبون (fāʾinna ḥizbu llāh hum al-ġālibūn) and means "Verily the members of the party of God are victorious," (Koran: 5:56).

Underneath the logo are the words المقاومة الإسلامية في لبنان (al-muqāwamah al-islāmīyah fī lubnān) or "The Islamic Resistance in Lebanon."

Since Hezbollah is based in Lebanon and has Arabic written on its flag, why is its name transliterated the Persian/Iranian way?

Because that's where Hezbollah came from in the first place: Iran.

This is the – overwhelmingly Shia – country where Hezbollah was first conceived by Muslim clerics as a militia to fight against the

Israelis following their 1982 invasion of Lebanon.

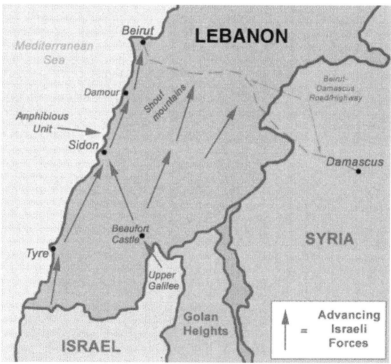

Hezbollah's leaders were followers of Ayatollah Khomeini...

...who had spearheaded the Islamic Revolution of 1979...

...overthrowing yet another of our Middle Eastern tyrannical protégés, the Shah of Iran...

...the ruler of one of the world's most unequal societies, where the poor lived in holes in the ground and his secret police, the SAVAK (see its seal below), murdered and horribly tortured tens of thousands.

Even though Israel's invasion of Lebanon is long over, Hezbollah's militia (which is also supported by Assad's Shi'ite regime in Syria), is still there to this day, waging guerrilla campaigns – and suicide bombings – against both Israel and the United States.

Witness the 1983 bombing of the U.S. Marine barracks in Beirut just to take one of many examples.

Hezbollah has become a state within a state in Lebanon. It has seats in the government, a radio and a satellite TV station, in addition to providing numerous social services, from hospitals, news services and schools…

...to soup kitchens.

It goes without saying that Hezbollah is immensely popular among Lebanon's Shi'ite community (40% of the population).

What is Hezbollah's relationship with ISIS?

It could hardly be worse. It's the Sunni/Shia thing again. Shia Hezbollah has vowed to defeat Sunni ISIS in Syria because ISIS is fighting against Shi'ite Assad…

…and has vowed to wipe out every other Shi'ite on the face of the earth, regardless of what group he or she might belong to. The two terrorist organizations are mutually exclusive.

   vs.

The only goal they have in common is the destruction of Israel.

(iii) Hamas

Hamas (Arabic: حماس *Ḥamās*) means "zeal" or "fighting spirit," but is also an acronym for حركة المقاومة الاسلامية *Ḥarakat al-Muqāwamah al-'Islāmiyyah* Islamic Resistance Movement), a Palestinian organization founded in 1988 in the West Bank and Gaza, but operating mainly out of Gaza in recent years.

Islamic Resistance, yes, but in spite of the Hamas flag (above) proclaiming that "There is no God but God. Muhammad is the Messenger of God," it must be said that the Palestinians, who are overwhelmingly Sunni, leavened by a small minority of Shi'ites and spiced by a sprinkle of Christians, are not particularly religious and in normal times couldn't tell you which of them was which, and cared less. (Which may explain why Sunni Hamas is funded by not only Sunni Saudi Arabia and Qatar, but also by Shia Iran and Hezbollah.)

Above all, the Palestinians are *geographical*, yearning for their lost land just as deeply as their "brothers," the Jews had yearned for theirs. (The Palestinians, like all Arabs and all Jews are brothers in language because both peoples speak Semitic languages – being "anti-Semitic" simply means you don't like people who speak Arabic or Hebrew).

Here is part of what the late Palestinian Poet Laureate, Mahmud Darwish, had to say about the Israeli-Palestinian situation, mesmerizing a typical 25,000-strong audience with a reading of his poem "He is calm" as he imagined himself sitting in a café with an Israeli:

He is calm and I am also
He is drinking tea with lemon,
And I am drinking coffee
This is the only thing that makes us different
Like me he wears a broad striped shirt
Like him I read the evening papers
He doesn't see my furtive glance
I don't see his furtive glance
He is calm and I am also

So where is Gaza? It's a little sliver of nothing much at all on the edge of Southern Israel...

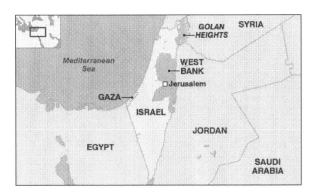

...covering a piddling 146 square miles. And yet it is one of the most densely populated places on earth, with a population of 1.6 million people crammed into a space the size of Philadelphia.

The Hamas seal contains much more information about the organization than its flag does.

The image of a map at the top of this design symbolizes that Hamas was founded to liberate Palestine from Israeli "occupation" and to establish an Islamic state in the area that is now Israel, including the West Bank and the Gaza Strip.

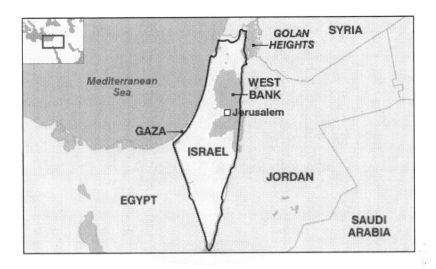

The image of a dome on the seal is the Muslim shrine, the Dome of the Rock in Jerusalem, which will be part of the liberation of Palestine.

To achieve their goal of regaining Palestine, Hamas established a military wing in 1991.

Hamas attacks on Israel from Gaza began in earnest in 2001. Between then and August 2014, almost 20,000 Hamas rockets hit southern Israel.

Israel responded with massive, deadly force over the same period.

The net result of this carnage according to the Israeli human rights group B'Tselem...

...was to cause 1,101 Israeli deaths and 7,065 Palestinian deaths, including the destruction of 20,000 Palestinian homes in Gaza...

...and the displacement of 500,000 Gazans.

In addition to its military wing, Hamas has a welfare wing providing social services to Palestinians in the Gaza Strip, including running relief programs...

...funding mosques, healthcare clinics, soup kitchens, sports leagues, orphanages and schools....

The work of Hamas in these fields supplements that provided by the United Nations Relief Works Agency (UNRWA).

On the other hand, Hamas's use of hospitals is sometimes criticized as serving to promote violence against Israel. Charities affiliated with Hamas are known to give financial support to families of Hamas militants who have been killed or imprisoned for carrying out military actions.

So Hamas does a lot of good in addition to doing a lot of bad. It's a very complicated picture.

What is Hamas's relationship with ISIS?

The Islamic State gave its answer to this question in June 2015 when it threatened to turn the Gaza Strip into another of its Middle East conquests, accusing Hamas of not being strict enough about religion.

"We will uproot the state of the Jews (Israel) and you and all of the secularists are nothing, and you will be over-run by our creeping multitudes," said an Islamic State spokesman in a video message addressed to the "tyrants of Hamas."

(iv) Taliban

Another of our creations, courtesy the Soviet invasion of Afghanistan in 1979. First, there was *al-Qaeda*, the CIA's very own database boys, and progenitors of ISIS, as we mentioned in Chapter 2, now it was the "students," from the Arabic *ṭālib*, the plural of which becomes *tālibān* طـالـبان in Pashto, one of the two official Afghan languages.

The name Taliban is supposed to stand for Students of Religion, since its members were originally "educated" in Sunni madrasas (religious schools) in Pakistan. We use the word "educated" advisedly, since their leader until he passed away recently was the one-eyed, semi-literate Mullah Muhammad Omar…

…and there is little evidence that the rank and file Taliban know anything about anything beyond parts of the Koran and some of the Hadith and the Sharia.

On that last count, there is not much to choose between the Taliban and ISIS in their disgusting treatment of women…

…and their sadistic punishments, reveling in precisely the same beatings…

...amputations...

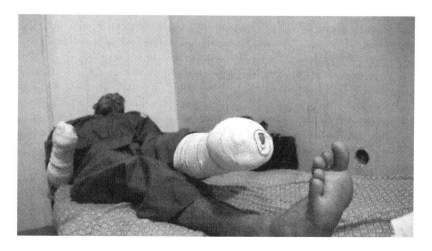

...and beheadings as the Islamic State...

Not to mention their love of destroying precious historic relics, such as the statues of the Buddhas of Bamiyan...

Islam vs. ISIS

The Taliban do have another claim to fame however that ISIS cannot compete with: they are the ultimate drug lords, presiding over 90% of all the opium production in the world, spread out all over Afghanistan and overlapping into Pakistan.

Large-scale cultivation of the opium poppy dates back to the British in India in the 1750s, who were to dominate the opium trade for the next 160 years, using Indian slave labor...

...to produce 13 million pounds of the narcotic annually in such giant arrays of mixing rooms and examining halls as this one...

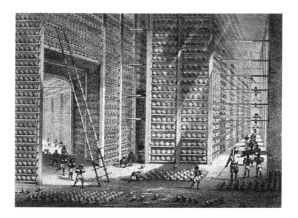

In the 1960s and 1970s, opium cultivation and trade shifted to Southeast Asia, a decade later to Turkey and Pakistan, and by the early eighties to Afghanistan.

Just in time for the Taliban to take full advantage of it.

Since 1979, the cultivation of opium – and manufacture of its derivatives, heroin and morphine – has skyrocketed. Amazingly, increasing even more rapidly after the US invasion of Afghanistan in 2001...

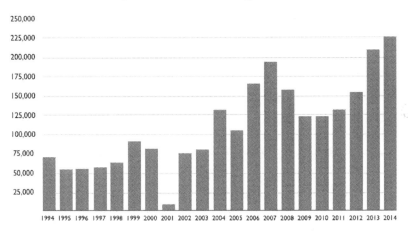

Hectares of opium cultivation in Afghanistan 1994-2014

...with almost 4,000 tons of the stuff exported every year, raking in about $4 billion, the lion's share of which goes to the Taliban.

But in spite of all their cruelty and greed, the Taliban are fierce fighters, which is precisely why the CIA provided them with huge amounts of arms and money to battle the invading Soviets alongside Osama's mujahideen, thereby creating a whole new breed of monsters.

Given all of the above, what sort of a relationship do you think the Taliban have with ISIS?

This recent picture provides the answer. It shows a line of Islamic State fighters forcing a group of blindfolded Taliban supporters to kneel unsuspectingly over buried devices set to blow them to pieces.

Why? Because, the Taliban made the fatal mistake of refusing to give in to the Islamic State's demand to take over their territories in Afghanistan and Pakistan, opium and all.

It remains to be seen when ISIS will make its move.

(v) Boko Haram

This is a 10,000 strong jihadist group based in northeastern Nigeria, but also active in Chad, Niger and northern Cameroon…

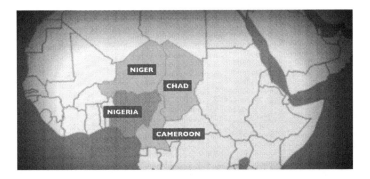

…an area measuring approximately 20,000 square miles, about the size of Belgium.

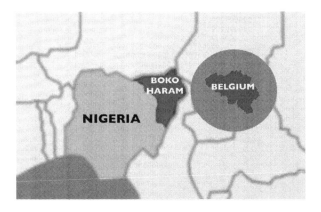

As of May, 2016, there have also been signs that Boko Haram jihadists are sending fighters to join ISIS in Libya, and of increased cooperation between the two groups.

The "Haram" in the name Boko Haram is Arabic for "forbidden" or "sin," and the "Boko" is a word in the Hausa language meaning "fraud" or "inauthenticity," but which is used by these terrorists as a synonym for "Western Education."

There's a catchy bumper sticker slogan for you:

Apart from its worship of the same pseudo-Islamic iron-age claptrap as ISIS, one of Boko Haram's favorite pastimes is kidnapping schoolgirls. One 1914 example of this involved 219 girls, aged 16-18, many of them Christian, and all taken from their school in the town of Chibok in northern Nigeria.

Since then, we have learned that many of the girls who were Muslim were brainwashed to flog other girls who couldn't recite the Koran, and even to slit the throats of Christian men Boko Haram came across. Many of the girls – Muslim or Christian – were also forced to marry the militants, whereupon they were repeatedly raped.

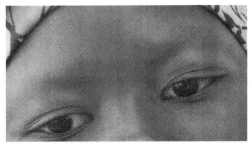

Just when it seemed that things couldn't possibly get any worse, they did – in the town of Baga, also in Northern Nigeria.

For five days, from the 3rd to the 7th of January 2015, Boko Haram attacked this tiny 3/4 of a square mile town, which was used by a multinational force that had been set up to fight them. Using petrol bombs and explosives, they burned down 620 structures...

...including all the – mainly Christian – people taking refuge inside them.

This was the largest massacre in Boko Haram's history, resulting in as many as 2,000 deaths.

ISIS would have been proud.

Which is precisely what Caliph Abu Bakr al-Baghdadi was to be two months later, when Boko Haram's leader, *Abu Bakr* Shekau (that name again) pledged his group's allegiance to the Islamic State.

(vi) Ash-Shabaab

The full name of this al-Qaeda affiliate group is حركة الشباب المجاهدين, Ḥarakat ash-Shabāb al-Mujāhidīn; The Mujahideen Youth Movement.

[Note the correct transliteration of this name as *ash-Shabāb*, since the Arabic letter *shin* is a Sun-letter, which assimilates the *al*]

Where do ash-Shabaab come from? Somalia.

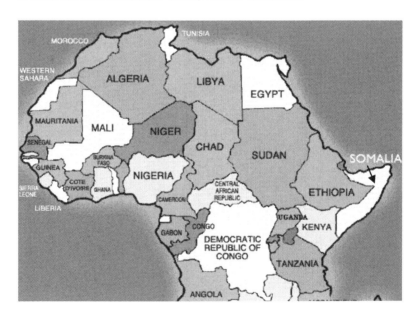

For most of us this name immediately conjures up images of pirates – especially if we've seen the movie, "Captain Phillips."

Does this mean that ash-Shabaab is involved with piracy? Yes and no.

In December 2010, ash-Shabaab took control of a pirate base run by another Somali Islamist group and apparently reached a compromise with the local pirate gangs that would give them a 20% share of all ransoms received from the hijacking of ships.

But that's not ash-Shabaab's main thrust, which is, first to establish an Islamic state in Somalia (99% Muslim), and eventually all across East Africa. To that end, the "Youth" have been launching hundreds of terror attacks over the last few years, not only on government forces in Somalia but also on neighboring African countries.

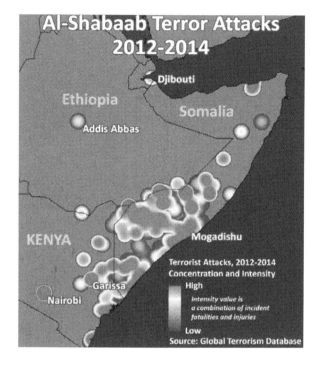

Notably in Kenya, partly in retaliation for that country's involvement in military action against ash-Shabaab in Somalia, and partly because 70% of Kenyans are Christian.

News of two of the most outrageous of these attacks echoed round the world.

The first of these was the 2013 attack on the Westgate Mall in Nairobi…

...which resulted in 67 deaths...

...and extensive damage...

The second major terror attack occurred in April of 2015 in northeast Kenya when ash-Shabaab invaded Garissa University College...

...and after a four-day siege ended up murdering 148 students...

In both cases – Westgate and Garissa – the gunmen asked every person they hadn't already slaughtered in their initial barrage to recite a passage from the Koran. If the person failed to do so, the terrorist shot him or her dead.

Now for our relationship-with-ISIS question. The latest news from ash-Shabaab – which commands around 9,000 fighters – was that ISIS had made overtures to the Somali group, but it has so far remained loyal to al-Qaeda.

Time will tell.

(vii) Quds Force

The Quds Force, from the Arabic *quds*, which means holy, or when written *al-Quds* signifies Jerusalem: the Holy City. In Persian, the Quds Force comes out as نیروی قدس.*Nīrū-ye Qods*, or سپاه قدس *Sepāh-e Qods*).

This is a special unit of Iran's Revolutionary Guards responsible for their foreign operations, reporting directly to the Supreme Leader of Iran, Ali Khamenei...

While "little is reliably known" about the force, the United States has declared it a terrorist organization since 2007. And it is indeed perhaps *the* most dangerous organization in the Middle East and Asia apart from ISIS, with operations in Europe, Russia, North America and India.

The Quds Force has about 15,000 troops, but we hear little about them engaging in direct action. Almost everything they do is obscure…

…or camouflaged…

The same applies to their ultra low-key "shadow" commander, Major General Qasim Soleimani…

...of whom a former C.I.A. officer in Iraq said, "He is the single most powerful operative in the Middle East – and no one's ever heard of him."

Why is this? Why is the "Jerusalem" Force and its mysterious "spymaster" commander so dangerous? What does it want?

The key is in their name. They want to turn Israel back into Palestine and retake the former's capital city, Jerusalem.

In the process, the Quds Force wants to take every opportunity to punish the U.S. for its support of Israel.

To that end, it connects with, maintains and supports every terrorist group in the region that will strengthen Iran and keep its enemies off balance.

And it is "sect-blind," straddling the Sunni-Shia divide to give money, arms and battlefield advice and military assistance to any organization that serves their purpose, whether it's Shia Hezbollah (a yearly donation of $100-200 million)...

…or Shia Assad (it's likely the Quds Force pushed Lebanese Hezbollah into Syria to buttress Assad)…

…or Sunni Hamas ("turn the land and sky into Hell for Israel")…

…or Sunni Taliban (military training)…

...or Sunni ash-Shabaab (organizing joint attacks)...

...or Sunni al-Qaeda under their current leader Ayman az-Zawahiri...

All of this makes the accelerating chaos in the Middle East even more confusing, with complexity piled upon complexity, aptly illustrated in the recent alliance formed between Russia, Shia Iran, predominantly Shia Iraq and Shia President Bashar Assad to battle Sunni ISIS, which is of course our own greatest enemy.

As the saying goes, the enemies of my enemy are my friends. Or are they?

Islam vs. ISIS

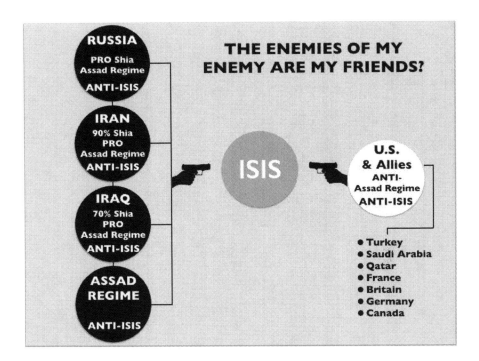

Speaking of ISIS, where does the Shia Quds Force stand vis à vis the Sunni Islamic State?

Apparently against it.

For now.

(viii) An-Nusra Front

We've already discussed the origins of al-Qaeda in Chapter Two. The organization now has the following direct affiliates:

- Al-Qaeda in Somalia (ash-Shabaab)
- Al-Qaeda in the Arabian Peninsula (Yemen)
- Al-Qaeda in the Islamic Maghreb (North Africa)
- Al-Qaeda in the Indian Subcontinent
- Al-Qaeda in Syria (an-Nusra Front)

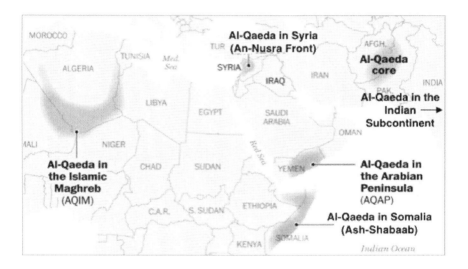

We've also already talked about the first two affiliates on this list. Now we'll jump to the last one: an-Nusra Front, or *Jabhat an-Nusra*, "Support Front" (Arabic: جبهة النصرة aka al-Qaeda in Syria.

[Note: just as in the case of ash-Shabaab, the correct transliteration of the name is *an-Nusra*, since like the Arabic letter *shin*, *nun* is a Sun-letter, which also assimilates the *al*]

Islam vs. ISIS

The Syrian Civil War has been going on since March 2011, pitting several hundred thousand troops loyal to President Bashar Assad...

...against an astonishing array of some 1,000 different rebel groups, numbering about 100,000 fighters in all, ranging from the most radical to the most moderate...

SYRIAN OPPOSITION EXTREMISM SPECTRUM

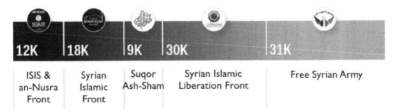

12K	18K	9K	30K	31K
ISIS & an-Nusra Front	Syrian Islamic Front	Suqor Ash-Sham	Syrian Islamic Liberation Front	Free Syrian Army

But how did this terrible war get started in the first place?

The trouble began in 2011 in the Syrian city of Deraa after 15 schoolchildren were arrested – and reportedly torture`d – for writing anti-government graffiti on the walls of a school...

...causing the people to take to the streets...

The community's outrage over the children's arrests and mistreatment emboldened and helped spread the Syrian opposition to Assad's vicious regime.

Syrians compare the dramatic dynamics in the rural city to the moment Tunisian street vendor Mohamed Bouazizi torched himself to death in December 2010...

Now for some background on the checkered careers of an-Nusra, al-Qaeda and ISIS during the last four years of war in Syria that have killed a quarter of a million people and left a further 16 million in need of assistance inside and outside Syria.

Here's the timeline:

- 2011: Upon the outbreak of the war, the leader of the Islamic State in Iraq, Abu Bakr al-Baghdadi and al-Qaeda authorize Abu Mohammad al-Jolani...

...to set up an affiliate called Al-Qaeda in Syria, or an-Nusra Front.
- 2012: an-Nusra now has about 10,000 fighters; 7% of the Free Syrian Army.
- 2013: Baghdadi splits from al-Qaeda and announces that he wants to merge an-Nusra and the Islamic State of Iraq into the Islamic State of Iraq and Sham, or ISIS.

An-Nusra + Islamic State of Iraq = Islamic State of Iraq and Sham = ISIS

Al-Jolani rejects the merger and affirms an-Nusra's continuing allegiance to al-Qaeda and its leader, Ayman az-Zawahiri, who has inherited the mantle from Osama bin Ladin...

Islam vs. ISIS

- 2014: Fighting breaks out between ISIS and an-Nusra, leaving hundreds dead on both sides. Al-Julani subsequently states, "There is no solution between ISIS and us."
- 2015: Dissension within the ranks of an-Nusra, with one camp wanting to keep its affiliation with al-Qaeda and a second camp wanting to break with al-Qaeda and go it alone.

Meanwhile, ISIS waits in the wings.

David Stansfield

10. How to defeat ISIS

As we saw in chapter 8, ISIS has recently lost a lot of territory in Iraq and Syria…

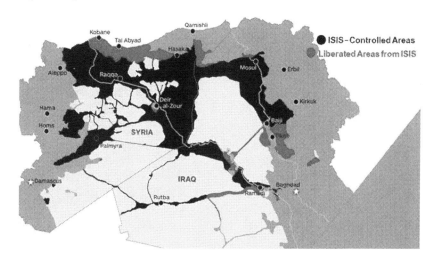

…but is compensating for this by encouraging small cells of lone wolf, home-grown terrorists across much of the world.

So, how to defeat this new metastasizing ISIS? Here are two ways that have been proposed to do this: a left-wing way and a right-wing way. Let's look at these two extremes of the political spectrum.

On the far left, we have Noam Chomsky, a world-renowned political dissident, linguist, author of over a hundred books and MIT professor emeritus. And on the far right, we have Max Boot, a military historian and the Jeane J. Kirkpatrick national security senior fellow at the Council on Foreign Relations.

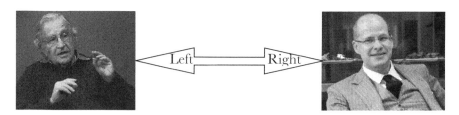

Islam vs. ISIS

Here's a condensed version of what Noam Chomsky had to say about defeating ISIS on the program, *Democracy Now*, March 3, 2015:

"It's very hard to think of anything serious that can be done. It should be settled diplomatically and peacefully to the extent that's possible, we should be getting together with (Shi'ite) Iran...

Barak Obama
President of the United States

Sayed Ali Khamenei
Supreme Leader of Iran

...which has a huge stake in the matter, and is the main force involved, and with the (predominantly Shi'ite) Iraqi government...

Barak Obama
President of the United States

Haider al-Abadi
Prime Minister of Iraq

...which is calling for Iranian support and trying to work out some arrangement which will satisfy the legitimate demands of the Sunni population, which is what ISIS is protecting and gaining their support from. ISIS is not coming out of nowhere. In Baghdad before the invasion, Sunni and Shi'a lived intermingled, they intermarried, they didn't even know if their neighbor was a Sunni or a Shi'a. You look at Baghdad today, it's segregated...

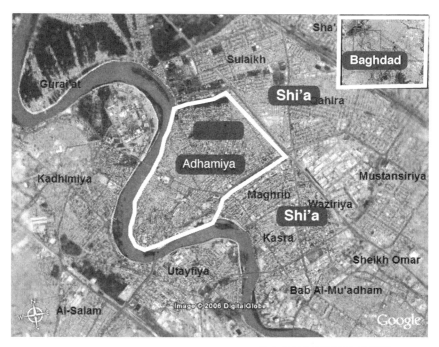

...a major Sunni-Shia conflict is rending the region apart, ripping it to shreds. This cannot be dealt with by bombs. This is much more serious than that."

Islam vs. ISIS

Now for the view from the right.

Here is a condensed version of Max Boot's *Council on Foreign Relations Policy Innovation Memorandum No. 51*, published November 14, 2014.

"To defeat ISIS, the president needs to dispatch more aircraft, military advisors, and special operations forces...

...and mobilize support from Sunnis in Iraq and Syria, as well as from Turkey, by showing that he is intent on deposing not only ISIS but also the equally murderous regime in Damascus."

"Specific steps include:

- Intensify air strikes.
- Lift the prohibition on U.S. boots on the ground.
- Increase the size of the U.S. force.
- Work with all of Iraq's and Syria's moderate factions.
- Send in the Joint Special Operations Command (JSOC).
- Impose a no-fly zone over part or all of Syria."

How did these two men's suggestions for defeating ISIS go down? Noam Chomsky's solution was completely ignored. Max Boot's solution was taken up with increasing vigor in recent months, but with decidedly mixed results, as we have seen.

So what *is* the solution? How do we defeat ISIS – and its genocidal accomplices, al-Qaeda, the Taliban, Boko Haram, ash-Shabaab and the rest of them? How do we stop the endless killing by these fanatical savages – spreading their poison all over the planet now – with the great majority of the victims being tens of thousands of Muslims? This isn't just the killing of people, which is bad enough; it is also the killing of the Islamic religion, giving it and its adherents the worse possible name and triggering widespread islamophobia.

What is the solution to this terrible problem?

It's been staring us in the face all along. The solution is Islam itself.

Only Islam can defeat the monster that is bent on destroying it. Which is to say that only the 99% of Muslims who condemn ISIS and company can wipe this abomination off the face of the earth, this contradiction of almost everything in Islam's Holy Book.

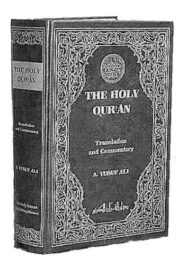

113 of the 114 surahs in the Koran begin with the words, "In the name of God, the *merciful* and the *compassionate*. Two adjectives that set the tone for everything Islam stands for.

It is no accident therefore that the Koran is at the heart of the Open Letter we mentioned in chapter 1...

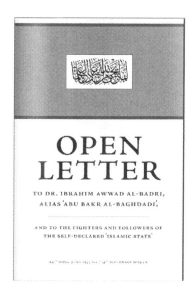

...the letter that nearly 200 Islamic scholars from every corner of the globe...

... addressed to the so-called "Caliph" al-Baghdadi of the so-called "Islamic State" in January 2014, methodically tearing every single thing this ghastly organization stands for to shreds.

Here are the key items in the Open Letter's list of actions that the Koran expressly forbids in Islam, every single one of which ISIS stands guilty of:

- *It is forbidden in Islam to kill the innocent.*
- *It is forbidden in Islam to kill emissaries, ambassadors, and diplomats; hence it is forbidden to kill journalists and aid workers.*
- *It is forbidden in Islam to harm or mistreat—in any way —Christians or any 'People of the Scripture'.*
- *The re-introduction of slavery is forbidden in Islam. It was abolished by universal consensus.*
- *It is forbidden in Islam to force people to convert.*
- *It is forbidden in Islam to deny women their rights.*
- *It is forbidden in Islam to deny children their rights.*
- *It is forbidden in Islam to enact legal punishments without following the correct procedures that ensure justice and mercy.*
- *It is forbidden in Islam to torture people.*

Mercy and compassion. It is this Koran, this Islam, that is the solution that has been hidden in plain sight all along. Only Islam itself can defeat the anti-Islam which is ISIS. Which is to say that if you are a moderate Muslim reading these words, part of the 99% who condemn the 1% that is ISIS, then the solution is YOU.

Only you as a member of the true Islam can defeat the horror that has the audacity to call itself the "Islamic State."

And precisely how will you go about doing this? Here are just a few obvious suggestions, but you will be able think of many more ways of flexing the muscles of your nearly 1.6 billion fellow Muslims:

BURY ISIS UNDER AN AVALANCHE OF SCORN
Turn every propaganda technique used by ISIS back on itself: the images, the videos, the video games, the radio and TV broadcasts, the movies, the hip-hop songs. Distribute anti-ISIS leaflets, pamphlets, slogans, books, newspapers, journals, CDs, DVDs, memory sticks. Publish your own multilingual anti-*Dabiq* magazine. Leave no publicity stunt unturned. Harness every possible medium of communication to trash the barbarians.

TWEET ISIS INTO OBLIVION
Twitter it and FaceBook it and YouTube it and Instagram it and Tumblr it and Flkr it and Flixster it and Pinterest it and WhatsApp it and Skype it and Pushover it and Wikileak it and text it and hashtag it and blog it and email it out of existence. Use every bit and byte of social media you can get your hands on. Bombard every newspaper and magazine and radio and TV outlet on the planet with Public Service Announcements and cries of outrage at what ISIS is doing to your religion.

BREAK THE ISIS CODE
Destroy ISIS communications worldwide via both the surface web and the Deep Web. Go viral with your viruses and malware and BitTorrent swarms and hash tables, infecting every ISIS computer and web connection and server in the land and eating up the bandwidths and protocols and databases of every ISIS IT network and file-sharing system with your worms, emptying their bitcoin accounts, bringing their

internet traffic to a shuddering halt, jamming their GPS systems, and reducing their video streams to a trickle and their domains to no man's lands.

HACK THE ISIS BANK ACCOUNTS TO PIECES
Phish the emails and phones of all the ISIS banks. Crash through their fire walls. Infiltrate their WiFi networks. Steal their usernames, passwords, and credit card details. Empty their ATMs. Bankrupt the bank robbers.

USE DRONES TO SPY ON ISIS
Make use of the latest hi-tech spy technology from virtual reality holograms to autonomous drones and microbots and quadcopters and hexacopters and GoPros and tiny electronic camera flies to detect and track and 3-D map and anticipate and foil ISIS's every move. (Note that there are enough brilliant techies and cybernauts in Muslim India alone –172 million followers of Islam – to accomplish all of the above with one hand tied behind their backs, using the algorithms and algebra that were yet other creations of the Golden Age of Islam and are still the foundation of digital technology today.)

STAGE MILLION MUSLIM MARCHES
Take to the streets of every Muslim country in your hundreds of thousands to besiege the mosques of pro-ISIS Mullahs. Block the traffic in the Islamic world's capital cities, demanding an immediate clamp-down on anyone who declares allegiance to ISIS. Organize worldwide parades, sit-ins, demonstrations, pickets, blockades and rallies along the same lines, with "Not in My Name" and "Muslims Against ISIS" posters, bumper stickers, placards and banners and slogans and t-shirts. Stage MASSIVE protests across the planet on a Gandhi/Martin Luther King/Mandela scale. All this includes establishing communication pyramids, selecting picket captains, preparing, distributing

and storing signs and banners, and organizing morale-boosting sessions to build up the protesters' resolve and solidarity.

LAUNCH A MUSLIM SPRING AGAINST ISIS
Start the Muslim chatter across the planet, using every mobile communication device known to man plus all the social networking services, from Linkedin and Vine and Google+ to Secret, Meetit, Disqus and Xing. See also Renren or 校内网, if you're one of the 100 million Chinese Muslims; VK, the largest European online social networking service – VKontakte or ВКонтáкте – if you're one of the 20 million Russian Muslims; Odnoklassniki or Одноклассники in Uzbekistan, Kyrgyzstan and Georgia; Cloob or شبکه اجتماعی کلوب if you're one of the 66 million Iranian Muslims. Compare blow-by-blow 24/7 notes on the campaign you are waging with fellow Muslims throughout the Islamic world. Occupy all the Tahrir Squares on earth.

You can think of much, much more. You have the power. You are 23% of the world, 99% of the true Muslims pitted against the 1% of false ones. If ever the odds were stacked in a people's favor in their battle against the evil that is ISIS, they are stacked in yours.

Consider what one little Muslim girl who had half her face almost blown away by a Taliban bullet has accomplished.

If Malala can persuade the Pakistan government to pass its first Right to Free Education Bill for all girls and boys, just imagine what nearly 1.6 billion Malalas could do.

You are the best hope for all of us.

Get together. Organize. There is enormous strength in your numbers.

Above all, do not be silent. Make yourselves heard.

Salaamu alaykum.

David Stansfield

islamversusisis@gmail.com

Made in the USA
Charleston, SC
01 October 2016